THE PRIESTHOOD OF THE BELIEVER

Dr. Sam Sasser & Dr. Judson Cornwall

The Priesthood of the Believer

Library of Congress Catalog Card Number: 98-074675

International Standard Book Number: 0-88270-765-5

Published by:

Bridge-Logos *Publishers*

1300 Airport Road, Suite E
North Brunswick, NJ 08902

Dedication

This book is dedicated to Sam Sasser from whose notes it was written. Dr. Sasser was an outstanding missionary, a pastor, a student, a convention speaker, and a faithful friend to thousands of us in the ministry of the Master. He is deeply missed here, but highly appreciated in Heaven and by his two children, Renee and Terry, who grew up on the mission field and in the church world as "the preacher's kids." Their own search for God has lead them into His heart and into full-time ministry in the harvest fields of the world. What greater joy could a mother and father have!

In Loving Memory

of my husband, Sam Sasser, who died on September 27, 1995. Though his body was weak, his spirit and deep longing to press on to know the Lord remained strong to the end. Many years of ministry were spent around tables of fellowship, in conferences, and in churches sharing the truths and the priority of our devotion and love for Christ through praise and worship.

As a servant of God and a minister of the Word in the United States and around the world, his life has left a legacy to our family and thousands of precious hearts. His infectious humor and joy in the midst of tribulation and heartache has kept many a day in perspective, reminding us that God reigns in and through it all.

He lives on in our memories and in our quest to know the Christ, whom he now worships face to face.

Flo Sasser

Contents

Acknowledgment

My deep gratitude goes to our friend and mentor Judson Cornwall, who so graciously consented to take Sam's materials and, adding his own insights, write this book. I remember the day in 1974 in Honolulu, Hawaii, when Dr. Cornwall shared the precious truth of the *Priesthood of the Believer* with our church. It ignited a fire in our hearts and a pursuit of God that glows brightly in my life today. His friendship, counsel, and influence has spanned the generations of the Sasser family. For his life, and the many hours spent to make this book a reality, I am forever grateful.

Flo Sasser

Preface

Sam Sasser was a friend of mine over many years. I ministered in two of his churches, and we shared convention ministries repeatedly. I seriously doubt if I ever heard him preach without weeping before God. He had such a precious, humble spirit and spoke with apostolic authority. When God promoted him to heaven, the family called on me to conduct his funeral.

Sam served as a missionary overseas for many years. When he returned to the United States, he enrolled in Fuller Seminary while pastoring a church in California. He wrote his doctoral thesis on the theme: *Worship, An Encounter With the Living God.* This became his theme for the rest of his ministry. He developed an amazing multi-media presentation on praise and worship and traveled extensively—sharing it with church congregations and convention delegates.

As his health began to restrict his traveling, he prepared a special teaching on the theme of *The Priesthood of the Believer* that was video taped and made part of the curriculum of Christian Life School of Theology, where he served as academic dean. The course has been distributed to hundreds of church Bible schools in America.

After Sam's death, his wife Flo approached me with an earnest plea to extract the course from the audio tapes and a syllabus and put it into book form so these truths could be shared with a wider audience. She brought me just about everything Sam had written on the subject of worship.

After investing many months digesting this material, I tried to write the book as a ghost writer. But I found myself incapable of duplicating Sam's style. When I offered the material back to Flo, she refused it and told me to write it as my book in my style of writing. "After all," she said, "He quoted you profusely."

This is what I have done. The material in this book is largely Sam Sasser's. Perhaps thirty percent of the material comes from me, but the style is entirely mine. I am a teacher. Sam was an exhorter. I took his exhortations and put them in a teaching format, often expanding it, but never violating Sam's point of view.

The Priesthood of the Believer is less a book about worship than it is a book about the worshiper. Sam believed, as I do, that every Christian has been invited into a priestly relationship with God. We offer unto the Lord the sacrifices of praise, and participate in leading others in their worship of God. This is a high and holy calling, but it is one seldom discussed in our churches. Perhaps it should be.

Judson Cornwall
Phoenix, Arizona
1998

1
The Extension of Priesthood
The Believer Priest

Why did God offer or extend to us the ministry of priesthood? God made no provision for a priesthood in the beginning. As long as Adam and Eve were in the garden, they did not need a priest. The Bible says: "*They* [Adam and Eve] *heard the voice* [NIV—*the sound*] *of the LORD God walking in the garden in the cool of the day.*"[1] The Adamses had an intimate, personal relationship with God. They walked and talked together in a knowing relationship, much as lovers can communicate without the use of words. The first couple had fellowship with the voice of the LORD.

This intimacy between God and Adam and Eve was more than an exchange of ardor or emotion. There was equally an impartation of knowledge. God was Adam's only teacher. Questions that send us to the *Encyclopedia Britannica* sent Adam to God. As long as Adam remained in intimate contact with God, his knowledge seemed unlimited. This was not the result of study. It was a spiritual ability to touch the mind of God. He had to be amazed at how smart God is.

We know little of that relationship. The Bible merely tells us that it existed. It may have been a communication of spirit to spirit rather than mind to mind. Perhaps it was a bit like the host computers (servers) that are on the Internet. Vast stores of knowledge are available to the home computer, one screen at a time. Adam was spiritually plugged into God. All the vast resources of God's knowledge were available to him as needed.

Unfortunately, Adam was not content with what was made available to him. He found only good on God's Internet. Satan insisted that the other half of the picture was to be found in evil. Adam succumbed to Satan's temptation to eat of the forbidden tree of the knowledge of good and evil in order to gain access to knowledge that God was withholding from him while awaiting sufficient maturity in Adam to handle it. Adam wanted it right now and he got it, but this sinful rebellion cost him his connection with God.

Just as being forced unexpectedly off the Internet produces a blank screen canceling all the information that had been available, so Adam found himself with a blank screen. Apparently nothing had been saved to his "hard disk," for when sin caused Adam's expulsion from the garden, he did not seem to retain much of what God had taught him.

What an emptiness Adam must have experienced. All his life he had enjoyed a spiritual intuitive knowledge that was not based on study or even on observation. Now he was, compared to days before, a blank. Whereas he used to look forward to walking and talking with God, now he feared God and hid himself from Him in the garden. Before sinning, Adam was completely open and transparent with God. Now he felt it necessary to cover himself with leaves—he felt naked for the first time in his life.

Something went wrong. Sin crashed the hard disk of his spirit. He could not call up the things for his use that he had previously learned from God. There was no "back-up" system for his spirit. The operating system of his mind still functioned, but years of truth that God had taught were unavailable to him. What a loss!

Sin Disconnects Us from God

When sin separates a person from God, and the Bible declares that it does, that individual cannot receive spiritual truth. Paul told the Corinthian church: "*The natural man does not receive the things of the Spirit of God, for they are foolishness to him; nor can he know them, because they are spiritually discerned.*"[2] The *Living Bible* translates this verse even more forcibly: "*The man who isn't a Christian can't understand and can't accept these thoughts from God, which the Holy Spirit teaches us. They sound foolish to him because only those who have the Holy Spirit within them can understand what the Holy Spirit means. Others just can't take it in.*"

To the unregenerate person, the voice of God is just so much noise. He or she may be able to learn law and principles from another person, but the Spirit of God lacks a channel through which to communicate to the unregenerate individual.

How painfully Adam learned this lesson. Flagrant disobedience cost Adam his home in the Garden of Eden and, far more important, his intimate relationship with God—his spiritual connection to God's Internet.

"But," you say, "God was merciful to Adam." Of course He was. God is merciful by nature. That is how He described Himself to be when Moses asked God to reveal Himself:

> *The LORD passed before him and proclaimed, 'The LORD, the LORD God, merciful and gracious, longsuffering, and abounding in goodness and truth, keeping mercy for*

> *thousands, forgiving iniquity and transgression and sin, by no means clearing the guilty. . . .'*[3]

This is how He has revealed Himself to humanity through all the ages—merciful, but just! Mercy does not overlook sin; it makes provision to bring persons out of that sin. This is what God did for Adam and Eve in the garden. He slew innocent animals as a substitute for the death our parents deserved, sprinkled blood over them, made coats from the skins to cover them, and instituted a sacrificial system of approach to God. The sin was atoned and the sinning ones were covered, but the damage from sin remained in Adam and Eve. They now had knowledge of good and evil[4] as a replacement for spiritual knowledge of God.

Whereas Adam and Eve had fellowship directly with the voice of God or the Spirit of God, they now had to fellowship through an innocent sacrifice. This called for someone to make the sacrifice, and that person was called a priest. The priesthood came into being to help restore fellowship between a person and his or her God.

As is all revealed truth, the understanding of a priest and priesthood is progressively revealed in the Bible. It is introduced in the book of beginnings, Genesis, but it is unfolded all the way to the book of Revelation. In this progressive revelation, it is easy to see seven levels of priesthood unveiled throughout the pages of God's Book as God sought to help persons get back online with God—to get back on God's Internet.

The Individual Priesthood

The first level of priesthood God instituted was the priesthood of each person. Although God Himself acted as priest in offering the first sacrifice for Adam and Eve, we never read of Him doing this a second time. It seems that God taught Adam to be his own priest, how to build an altar, what was acceptable as a sacrifice, how to offer it to God, and how, through this, to find acceptance and limited access to God. Adam, in turn, taught this to his sons.

God knew, far better than we do, how very personal the act of worship is. Although the worshiper was having to approach God through the sacrificial system, God let it be a very personal act. Chapter 4 of Genesis pictures Cain and Abel offering individual sacrifices before God. Every indication is that each acted as the priest—the one doing the offering—for his sacrifice. Each was both the suppliant and the sacrificer.

How convenient! How personal! Its individuality is easily seen in Abraham's obedient response to sacrifice Isaac at God's command. He left the servants at the base of the mountain and took only his son and the wood to the place of sacrifice God had appointed. The issue was strictly between God and Abraham. There was no mediating priest available to him. Abraham was first of all a priest unto himself, then a priest to his household. Before the sacrifice was ever offered, God intervened and provided a ram as a substitute for Isaac. God had no desire for human sacrifice. He was testing Abraham's level of obedience and allowing this patriarch to discover that his great love for his son had not replaced his deep devotion to God.

The principle of each person acting as his own priest was not long lived. Very early in the program Cain decided to change the rules to fit his situation. To offer God an animal from the flock, as God had specified, Cain had to negotiate with his shepherd brother, Abel. Cain was a farmer, not a shepherd. Somehow it seemed unreasonable not to be allowed to give God the increase of his labor. Lacking spiritual understanding, Cain functioned in human reasoning and offered vegetables to God. The sacrifice was disallowed by God.

When Cain saw God's approval on his brother's sacrifice of an animal, jealousy and eventual hatred welled up in him. Perhaps he could see some future power of control in his younger brother who had a monopoly on the supply of animals acceptable for sacrifice. Cain murdered his brother in a fit of rage and buried his body, but God was looking.

This rebellion against God's prescribed way of approaching Him became so widespread that by the time of Adam's death, there were but a handful of persons who still observed the sacrificial system and sought to contact God. In the entire genealogical list of Adam, we come to Enoch before any mention is made of a person having contact with the living God, and Enoch was born nearly 60 years after Adam died.

Wickedness was so rampant in the world that:

> *The LORD was sorry that He had made man on the earth, and He was grieved in His heart. So the LORD said, "I will destroy man whom I have created from the face of the earth, both man and beast, creeping thing and birds of the air, for I am sorry that I have made them."*[5]

We know the outcome of this heartbreak—God's judgement came in the form of a flood that destroyed all mankind except Noah and his household. The individual priesthood failed through disobedience to God's prescribed way. "I'd rather do it my way" seemed to prevail over doing it God's way. That is still a dangerous temptation today.

The Father Priesthood

The second level of priests God instituted to bring persons back into spiritual relationship with Himself is the father priest. The oldest book of the Bible is Job. We're not certain where to place him in the list of patriarchs, but he antedates most of them. Early in this book, Job is pictured as the priest of his family.

We read:

> *So it was, when the days of feasting had run their course, that Job would send and sanctify them, and he would rise early in the morning and offer burnt offerings according to the number of them all. For Job said, "It may be that my sons have sinned and cursed God in their hearts." Thus Job did regularly.*[6]

Job didn't wait for his children to reach out to God. He approached God on their behalf. He was the priest of the home. He set the spiritual tone, and He offered the sacrifices unto God.

This father priesthood characterized the patriarchal era. The family was the governmental unit of those generations. Few people lived in communities. They were farmers, cattlemen, and shepherds. The family looked to the father as the ultimate authority figure of their world and, as such, it was natural that he would be their access to God.

Happy is the home that has a father priest. What security against satanic attacks it affords. Access to God doesn't require a church—the home is a wonderful place to talk with God, and children can so easily be brought into communion with God when the father of the home accepts that responsibility and exerts spiritual leadership. Even in the New Testament, we see God expecting the father to function as the priest in his home. Like Job, we can intercede for our children as well as introduce them to God individually.

The Tribal Priesthood

God's third level of priesthood was the tribal priesthood. The father priest worked quite well as long as the family wasn't scattered too widely, but growth forced separation for survival.

As the lineage of Abraham increased in numbers, they related to one another by tribal membership. Families found identification in the larger unit. During their captivity in Egypt, the Hebrews kept their identity by maintaining tribal classifications. These were so defined and strong that when God marched them out of Egypt, He led them by tribes. God directed them to camp by tribes, and when they entered the Promised Land, they received their inheritance by tribes.

It is very likely that Melchisedec was a tribal priest. Jethro, the father-in-law of Moses, is called the priest of Midian in Exodus 3:1, and the book of Judges speaks of tribal priests. Moses treated the head of each of the twelve tribes of Israel as the priest of each tribe.

Although the priesthood of the father was never totally terminated until the Aaronic priesthood was established, it became more practical for the head of each clan or tribe to function as the priest for his tribe. It was a new unit of government for the enlarging nation, and God wanted its leaders to direct the people to Himself. These tribal priests were connecting links to God. Do I dare liken them to web browsers that link the computer to the Internet?

Perhaps we could apply this to the position of pastors of congregations. They have individual families gathered together in a special "clan," and they are expected to function as a priest on behalf of God and the people. It is a high and holy calling to be entrusted with the spiritual life of individuals and families. God treats it very seriously. Perhaps we should, too.

No pastor should play "god" to a congregation, but all pastors should become priests unto God and unto the congregation. That is, the pastor brings the presence and words of God to the people, and he leads the congregation into the presence of God.

The National Priesthood

Almost nothing that God gets involved in remains small. Where there is life, there is growth and multiplication. This certainly proved to be true with the family of Abraham after God blessed him. The family became a tribe and under Jacob it divided into twelve family tribes. These tribes became a nation. The priesthood had to grow, too. The fourth step in the development of priesthood was the institution of a national priest.

When God brought His people out of Egypt, they may have traveled as tribes, but they were becoming a nation. The tribes were losing some of their individuality as they merged into the larger identity of a nation. To help bring this larger unit into a proper relationship with God, Moses functioned for several years as the national priest. He became their intercessor. He took their place before God, and he led the people in their devotion to God. He received the words of God and shared them with the people. He taught them the laws of God, and led them in the construction of a tabernacle to house the presence of God. He was to the nation what Job had been to his family—a priest.

Many years later, during a severe spiritual decline in Israel, God raised up Samuel to function as a national priest. He was not of the family of Aaron nor of the priestly tribe of Levi. He was an Ephramite. God had accepted him as his mother's gift to become a servant to the high priest Eli. When in one day Eli and his priestly sons died, God elevated Samuel to function as the priest for the nation. He offered the sacrifices, taught the Law, judged persons from the law, and anointed Israel's first king. Samuel was a faithful prophet/priest. He knew the voice of God, and he knew how to approach God. He is a grand picture of what God desires in national leaders.

As many of the kings of Israel and Judah demonstrated, it is easy to be so overwhelmed with authority and power as to step aside from God's Word and become a law unto oneself. The old adage, "Power tends to corrupt; absolute power corrupts absolutely," has proven to be universally true. The combination of priest/king has consistently been difficult to find. How wonderful it would be if the world leaders of today were also priests unto the most high God. Our nations could again be returned to righteousness. We could again get signed on to God.

The Aaronic Priesthood

God's fifth step in establishing a reunion with Himself and His unlimited resources was the Aaronic priesthood. Both Moses and Samuel found being a national priest a heavy burden. This was especially true of Moses who had the entire government of Israel on his shoulders. He was responsible to make free men out of slaves. These people had been in slavery for over 300 years. They didn't have a clue how to function as free moral agents. It reminds me of a person redeemed from the enslavement of sin. He needs time to learn to live in the freedom of God's grace.

God's earthly government was best expressed in the balance of a prophet, priest, and king. When one man was all three, the balance was lost and the burden became unbearable. God saw that

Moses needed help, so He determined to relieve Moses of the responsibility of being the priest for this nation. Instead, He chose Aaron, the brother of Moses, to be consecrated to the office of High Priest.

The government God instituted for Israel was centered around the law that was given on Mt. Sinai. In that law, God made provision for a rather elaborate system of worship that involved the construction of the tabernacle. All of Israel's worship took place at this site.

The worship ceremonies and rituals of the tabernacle were far too involved and elaborate for an individual or father priest to perform. God chose Aaron and his sons to fill this office, and He rigorously prepared and trained them. When two of those sons, Nadab and Abihu, substituted their own altars to offer sacrifice before God, God slew them with fire from heaven. This so depleted the priesthood that God chose the entire tribe of Levi to act as assistants to Aaron. They moved from Israel's encampment and pitched their tents around the Outer Court of the tabernacle.

The priests were especially consecrated to the office. No one could volunteer to serve as a priest. They underwent ceremonial cleansing, and God clothed them with vestments that set them apart from the worshipers. They were a called out, consecrated group of persons. Their service was for men unto God. They made the sacrament of forgiveness available to sinning persons, and they offered the praise and worship of the forgiven ones back to God.

God's provision of a multiple priesthood, governed by the High Priest, placed the position of priesthood at its highest level until the coming of Christ. Only Moses and the Law were more highly revered by the Jews than the high priests. There were seasons in Jewish history when the priests were the rulers of the people. Other times the High Priest was the ruling power behind the king. One can hardly think of Israel without envisioning the priesthood, for access to the covenants of God were through their service and ministry. They were a growth replacement for the preceding four levels of priesthood. The priesthood was growing up!

The Worldwide Priesthood of Jesus

The Aaronic priesthood served the nation of Israel admirably, if not perfectly, but the New Testament boldly teaches what the Old Testament merely hinted at: "*God so loved the world . . . .*"[7] If God was to reunite peoples of all races, tribes, nations, and languages back into a flow of fellowship with Himself, He would need a world-wide priest. This sixth level of priesthood found its fulfillment in Jesus Christ, the Son of God.

In my earlier book, *Let Us Draw Near*,[8] I point out that everything in the tabernacle spoke of Jesus. All dimensions, materials, placement of furniture, and utilization of the services of the tabernacle are direct types of Jesus. While God had Israel construct a tabernacle as a place where the priests could serve for the entire nation, John tells us, "*The Word became flesh and dwelt among us, and we beheld His glory, the glory as of the only begotten of the Father, full of grace and truth.*"[9] The Greek word we have translated here as "dwelt" is *skenoo* which means "to tent or encamp." Some translations say, "*The Word . . . tabernacled with us.*" Jesus was not only God's High Priest here on earth, He was equally the meeting place for God and man. "*He tabernacled with us.*"

The book of Hebrews delights in telling us that Jesus was better than Aaron and the entire priesthood of Israel. Whatever imperfections belonged to the Aaronical high priesthood were not to be found in Jesus, and a variety of excellencies are to be found in Jesus that none of the high priests of the Old Testament lineage possessed.

Jesus was not only the tabernacle and the priest of the tabernacle, He was the sacrificing High Priest and the sacrifice. He became our substitute as well as our intercessor. We are redeemed not only because Jesus made a great offering as our priest, but because He was the sacrifice that was offered. John introduced Jesus to the multitudes with the prophetic declaration, "*Behold! The Lamb of God who takes away the sin of the world,*"[10] and the book of Revelation refers to Him as "*the Lamb slain from the foundation of the world.*"[11] No Old Testament priest could have done this; no New Testament believer priest can do it either. It is unique to the priestly ministry of Jesus.

An additional particularity in the priestly ministry of Jesus is that it has never ceased. Throughout the Old Testament, men could serve as a priest only while they lived. Death obviously canceled their appointment. Of Jesus we read, "*Therefore He is also able to save to the uttermost those who come to God through Him, since He always lives to make intercession for them.*"[12] Christ's sacrifice of Himself was done once and for all. It never needs to be repeated, but His ministry of intercession in heaven is eternal in nature. There is no time line to the High Priestly office and ministry of Jesus. There is no exhaustion level in Him. We never need worry that He will resign— "*He always lives to make intercession for them.*" Hallelujah!

The Believer Priesthood

The seventh level of priesthood is the priesthood of the believer, for as glorious as the ascension of Jesus was, it left the earth without a visible priest. True, some remnants of the first five levels of priesthood can still be found in limited locations, but Jesus supplanted all previous priesthoods. The blood of Jesus Christ made full atonement for all sin, so no earthly priest is needed to offer sacrifices or seek to obtain expiation for sin. The sin question was settled once and forever at Calvary. John assures us, "*If we confess our sins, He is faithful and just to forgive us our sins and to cleanse us from all unrighteousness.*"[13] While the Old Testament priest could, through the God ordained ordinances, atone for (cover) sin, Jesus doesn't merely cover sin, He cleanses us from all the unrighteousness that sin had imposed upon us and completely forgives that confessed sin. In a very literal way, we are "unsinned" by the sacrifice of Jesus Christ. This priestly ministry was completed by Jesus. It is over—never to be repeated.

It would seem, then, that the priestly ministry became antiquated at the ascension of Jesus, but that is not so. Remember that the Old Testament priest had a triple function: he brought God's atonement for sin to persons, he interceded on behalf of the people according to the will of God, and he directed the admiration response of these persons to God.

The priestly function of atonement is over because of the complete work of Christ Jesus, but Jesus still needs believer priests who will join Him in making intercession for others according to God's revealed will. The greatest need in the believer priest is to administer responses from redeemed persons back to God. That is what God has provided in His believer priests. He has commissioned individuals who are connected to God to lead the worship on earth.

The cycle of the priesthood has made a complete circuit. It began with the individual priesthood, and it ends with the individual believer's priesthood. In the New Testament, the Apostle Paul asks: "*Do you not know that you are the temple of God and that the Spirit of God dwells in you?*"[14] Much as Jesus "*tabernacled among us*" as a meeting place with God, so we "tabernacle" in this world as the dwelling place of God and the meeting place of men and God. We are redeemed to be houses of God's presence and places for man's worship.

When John was caught into heaven, he heard a declaration, "[*Jesus Christ*] . . . *has made us kings and priests to His God and Father, to Him be glory and dominion forever and ever. Amen.*"[15] Jesus has made *us*, the redeemed individuals, to be functioning priests here on earth.

Peter had a grasp on this truth, for he wrote, "*But you are a chosen generation, a royal priesthood, a holy nation, His own special people, that you may proclaim the praises of Him who called you out of darkness into His marvelous light.*"[16]

Adam and Eve were gloriously connected to God so that all of God's nature was available to them. Through our priestly position, we are now reconnected to God to both receive from Him and to give unto Him. What a glorious ministry God has made available to us!

Chapter 1 Endnotes

1. Genesis 3:8
2. 1 Corinthians 2:14
3. Exodus 34:6-7
4. See Genesis 4:22
5. Genesis 6:6-7
6. Job 1:5
7. John 3:16
8. Judson Cornwall, *Let Us Draw Near*, Bridge-Logos Publishing Company, South Plainfield, NJ, 1977
9. John 1:14
10. John 1:29
11. Revelation 13:8
12. Hebrews 7:25
13. 1 John 1:9
14. 1 Corinthians 3:16
15. Revelation 1:6; 5:10
16. 1 Peter 2:9

2
The Enterprise of Priesthood
The Believer Priest's Responsibility

What a glorious ministry God has made available to us, indeed! Not only are we called "*Sons of God*,"[1] we have been made "*Priests unto God*."[2] In a very real way, we have been saved to serve. Throughout the revelation of the New Testament, this emphasis is clear. Paul declares: "*We, who were the first to hope in Christ, might be for the praise of his glory.*"[3] Weymouth's translation clarifies this: "*That we should be devoted to the extolling of His glorious attributes*."[4] The Knox New Testament says, "*We were to manifest His glory,*"[5] and the Twentieth Century New Testament translates it, "*That we should enhance His glory.*"[6] It is indisputable that we have been saved to worship, and to lead others into the worship of God. This is the destiny of a believer priest—thanksgiving, praise, and worship.

This may be our destiny, but it has its challenges and hardships. It will be a true enterprise for each of us to bring ourselves into worship first of all, and then to lead others into this wonderful ministry of the redeemed. Webster's Dictionary defines enterprise as (1) "*A project or undertaking that is difficult, complicated, or risky.*" (2) "*Readiness to engage in daring action.*"[7] Any attempt to bring worship back to our churches will be difficult, complicated, and risky. The believer priest must be prepared to engage in daring action. His or her task is an enterprise of the first magnitude, but since the Lord Who assigned it, "*ever liveth to make intercession for us,*"[8] the assignment is accomplishable. God is counting on His believer priests to keep worship alive in every generation.

Church history shows that true, pure worship seldom passes from one generation to another. The forms and rituals of expression are handed down, but the heartfelt devotion to God that lies at the heart of worship must be discovered by each succeeding generation. Although worship is as old as Adam and Eve, it requires a personal and intimate relationship with God to prime the expression of worship from a person.

Robert Webber says: "One of the most serious needs in the Church today is the rediscovery of biblical worship. Many Church leaders recognize this and are calling the Church to a renewed concern for worship."[9] He emphasizes the gravity of the problem in the following quote:

> The area in which the least reform has taken place among us is in our corporate worship life. Through an unofficial survey, I discovered that the majority of evangelical lay people don't have the foggiest notion of what corporate worship really is. To questions such as: Why does God want to be worshiped? What is the meaning of an invocation or benediction? What does reading the Scripture, praying or hearing a sermon have

> to do with worship? I received blank stares and bewildered looks.[10]

This statement, which appeared in a monthly evangelical magazine, concluded: "Part of the problem is that we have made our churches into centers of evangelism and instruction. The focus of our services is on man and his needs instead of God and his glory."[11]

The ministry of worship in its purest form directs its attention and focus on the person of God. All other pursuits are clearly on the periphery of our service. *The Biblical Illustrator*, speaking of the "power to worship our Creator," asserts:

> All men have this; but in many it exists only in a latent state. Thousands of human souls are nothing better than the burial places of their own faculties. It seems as if some malignant spiritual magician had waved his terrible wand over human nature, causing a deep sleep to fall upon its noble instincts and thus preventing its development. One of the greatest dangers of the present time is the weakening of this power in men. The heathen worshiped senseless idols; the Ancient Greeks worshiped beauty; in the days of chivalry men worshiped physical strength, military dignity, valor, and courage; but the tendency of many in our age is to worship nothing. Even in the church the idea of worship does not occupy the place it did in other times. The leading conception appears to be preaching.[12]

A crisis of imminent proportion exists in today's Church world. Busyness in "doing something for God" has deceitfully replaced our pursuit of God. Our service for God is not proof of our love for God. Many persons serve out of duty or a desire to be rewarded. Others enter the "service of God" for ego satisfaction and to enjoy the praise of others. It would take a vivid imagination to see this as biblical worship of God.

Service may flow out of a love motivation, but it is not a producer of that love. Worship service flows out of a heart that is caught up with and focused on the object of its affection. For instance, the husband intending to express his love for his wife through service (doing the dishes, taking out the garbage, etc.) will soon discover that these acts in themselves, while appreciated, are insufficient to meet the real needs of his wife. Until he takes his wife into his arms and sincerely and intimately expresses his love to her, he leaves her unfulfilled and insecure. After he has made her secure in his love, any act of service he may offer is seen as a further expression of his love. Similarly, it is only when Christian service is an outflow of our deep love for God that it enters the realm of worship.

In my first book I wrote:

> Worship first, service second. Until we have fulfilled the worship requirement, we cannot serve properly. All service must flow out of worship lest it become a substitute for worship. We long ago learned that God will curse a substitute, but may bless a supplement . . . it is not an "either/or" situation, but "both/and." We will both worship and serve the Lord God, but in that order.[13]

Roxanne Brant, a student at Harvard Divinity School, Boston University School of Theology, and a graduate from Gordon Divinity Schools, speaks forcibly to this issue in writing:

> One of the main reasons for the power failure today in the Christian Church is that Christians have failed to minister to the Lord. Biblically the evidence is that our ministry to the Lord must come before our ministry to men if we are to be effective. Even after being filled with the Holy Spirit, if our priorities regarding these two types of ministry are reversed, we will be helpless and impotent before the heathen world. We need to once again dig down into the springs of God's life and bury ourselves in Him, The Source. We need to be caught up in the wonder of the person of Jesus Christ of Nazareth, to know Him intimately and deeply: then we will find

that our ministry Godward will urge us manward with a new freshness and power, and then we will not only talk of God's power but will also see it demonstrated.[14]

Activity can become an enemy of adoration as surely as service can become a substitute for submission and supplication. Our human nature is more comfortable with doing for God than being with Him.

What is Worship?

If religious activity is not worship, what is true worship? We can get the secular view from the dictionary that defines worship as: "reverence tendered a divine being; an act of expressing such reverence, to regard with extravagant respect honor or devotion."[15] The dictionary lists the following twelve words as either analogous words for worship or synonyms of worship: *adore, admire, dote, esteem, exalt, love, magnify, regard, respect, revere, reverence,* and *venerate.* Quite obviously, worship is totally concerned with the worthiness of God, not the worthiness of the worshiper.

Christian writers and speakers have described worship in many different ways. Gibbs calls it the "overflow of a grateful heart, under a sense of Divine Favor."[16] Bloomgren says that worship is "man's response to God's revelation of himself."[17] I have consistently defined worship as "love responding to love."[18] Worship has been interpreted in more intimate expressions ranging from intercourse to involvement. Taylor insists that worship will also include an outreach to the unregenerate.[19]

To worship God is to ascribe to Him supreme worth, for He alone is worthy. Our present day English word came from the Anglo-Saxon "*weorthscipe*." This meant to attribute worth to an object of affection. Two prominent terms used in the richness of interpretive worship in the Old Testament give keen insight. The Old Testament first gives us the Hebrew word "*hishahawah*." This means "a bowing down," and is indicative of the strong emphasis that Israel placed on respect and humility when approaching God. The expression was used for revering and showing the utmost in respect for one's leaders.[20] It reached its greater and richer meaning when emphasizing the Hebrew approach to God.[21] The Septuagint version of the Bible that translated the Old Testament into Greek translates the Hebrew word *shahah* with the Greek word *proskunein* that means "to stoop low and kiss in deep respect."[22] This is the most frequent word used for worship in the New Testament.

The Hebrews also referred to worship with the term *Abodah* that is frequently translated "service." Its root is derived from the word for "slave" or "servant"—*ebed.* Fuller Seminary's Doctor Ralph Martin, stresses the importance of this concept of worship in writing:

> . . . the highest designation of the Hebrew in his engagement with the worship of God is just this word, "servant." He delighted to call himself God's "*ebed*," (e.g., Psalm 116:16), and expressed that joy in his acts of private and corporate praise and prayer. Unlike the Greek thought of slavery as servile abasement and captivity, the Hebrew nation, implicit in the word, "*ebed*," expressed the relationship of servant and kindly master, (e.g., Exodus 21:1-6). This bond was thought of and described in terms of privilege and honor . . . and when men called themselves the "servants of God" in the cultic sense, they were paying tribute to the intimate and honored relationship into which God had brought them.[23]

The Scripture then speaks of Israel's great leaders as "*The Servants of God.*"[24] The corresponding word in the Greek language is "*latreia*" meaning service. Paul uses this word to mean the intimacy and honor of the solemn privilege of "*offering.*"[25] These definitions bring the concept of worship into an appropriate sense of reverence, relationship, and response.

After reading thousands of pages of research into the historical evidence of the great days of revival, Sam Sasser was convinced that the Church must return to the basics of worship if we are to experience revival in our generation. Only God can revive His Church, and we believer priests must press onward to renewed intimacy with God. The twin ministries of prayer and praise are alternate heartbeats that bring us into the divine presence. The Church will experience heart failure without them.

Why the Crisis?

If the prevailing crisis in our churches is the lack of heartfelt worship, we need to ask ourselves "Why?" How did we get into this work-oriented mentality? Why have we built places of worship and failed to use them for worship? Perhaps our priests and pastors have forgotten their *ebed* relationship to God and have become servants of themselves or the people.

For many years there has been increased emphases on pulpit ministry in both the fundamental and evangelical churches. All other parts of what is termed "the worship service" are referred to as "preliminaries." This has turned the attention of the worshipers from Christ to the preacher or the preaching. Neither of these are apt objects of our worship. Leonard Ravenhill warns:

> One does not need to be spiritual to preach, that is to make and deliver a sermon of homiletical perfection and exegetical exactitude. By a combination of memory, knowledge, ambition, personality, plus well lined bookshelves, self-confidence and a sense of having arrived . . . brother, the pulpit is yours almost anywhere these days. Preaching of the type mentioned affects men; prayer affects God. Preaching affects time; prayer affects eternity. The pulpit can be a shop window to display our talents; the closet speaks death to display.[26]

The pressure and cares of daily living have taken a toll on the attention span and maturation of the normal twentieth century believer. The mind wanders with changing interests. Adaptations are demanded by a wearied congregation and the anxious, worn clergy respond to these demands. The gathering of God's people for worship takes on a "quick order" mentality. Jesus spoke of this when He said, "*The care of this world and the deceitfulness of riches, choke the Word, and he becometh unfruitful*."[27] Christ cautioned us to "*take heed of yourself lest at any time your heart be overcharged with surfeiting and drunkenness and the cares of this life so that day come upon you unawares.*"[28] The prophet Daniel points decisively to the satanic plan when speaking of the anti-Christ and declares, "*And he shall speak great words against the Most High and shall wear out the saints of the Most High.*"[29]

A weary, worn out, and care-filled Church faces the end of this twentieth century. Spiritual infantile paralysis has seized and crippled great segments of the Body of Christ. This is a paradox, indeed. The Body of Christ—the healer—crippled? Obviously! In many areas the Church appears "spastic" in action—uncoordinated with its spiritual head, the Lord Christ. It functions as though Jesus was still in the tomb.

Any effort on the part of the Church to shake herself and move out of the danger of this twilight into the warmth of a spiritual noonday sun is met with caution. Leadership exhorts, "Let's not become so heavenly minded that we are of no earthly good," but even the most infantile of believers can see that the Church is not, by and large, suffering from such an undue heavenly complex. It is more that we are so earthy minded that we are of no heavenly good.

The restoring ministry of the Spirit is more than the anointed preaching of sound doctrine, although doctrine is vital. We must allow the Holy Spirit to bring us back to an intimate relationship with our God. Leonard Ravenhill clarifies this distinction in writing:

> We need a vision of a Holy God. God is essentially holy. The Cherubim and Seraphim were not crying, "Omnipotent! Omnipotent! Omnipotent is the Lord." Nor, "Omnipresent and Omniscient is the Lord," but, "Holy! Holy! Holy!" This Hebrew concept needs to penetrate our souls again.[30]

Surely today's Church needs an emphasis that will act as a catalyst for revival, and this is where the emphasis must be. The urgency of the hour demands that the Church be involved in a renewed intimacy with a Holy God. Problems that hinder such participation must be solved.

Howard Moody comments:

> Our worship is non-participatory performance ordered and planned to perfection, guaranteed not to challenge or embarrass or involve the observer beyond the limits of his rational comprehension . . . Christian worship is full of symbols that have been tamed and domesticated so as not to disturb our feelings or our lifestyle. The images we employ have been trivialized and there is present no symbol of reality that captures our minds and captivates our spirits so that our bodies move with a new purpose in this world.[31]

An uneasy feeling prevails in the Church. Something isn't right! The shepherd faults the sheep for not following; the sheep fault the shepherd for not leading. This dilemma is not new. Charles Finney, in writing to pastors and Church leaders in his day, carefully instructed them with the words, "Now dearly beloved brethren, unless there is a spirit of a revival in the ministry, it is vain to expect it in the church. The proper place for the shepherd is before or in advance of the sheep."[32]

Many pastors and spiritual leaders are aware of the spiritual insufficiency of most churches. Some are very innovative in seeking ways to overcome this deficiency while others beat old drums and sing worn out themes. Six of the most often proposed answers to the lack of spiritual vitality are: work, Bible study, missions, community, spiritual warfare, and prayer meetings. All these are laudable endeavors and probably have a place in the life of a church, but they can only express life—they cannot produce it. Look at these attempts.

Work

The church leader, knowing something must be done, organizes "work" opportunities. He supposes that it's the busy churchman that is the happy churchman. It is amazing the number of work opportunities some leaders can create, but often little interest is shown by members of the congregation, and those who respond are left empty in their spirits. Perhaps these leaders need to read what Jay B. Oaks wrote:

> Works find their proper place in spiritual properties. All who minister unto the Lord in praise as top priority find more effectiveness for remaining tasks. The weary shepherds and sheep need to turn "faces thitherward" and join themselves together to the Lord.[33]

Such exhortation, however, leaves the church leader still second-guessing. "But I am joined to the Lord," he reasons. "I'm looking to Him daily. My faith is solid and my confession positive."

Bible Study

Quite naturally, the church leader assumes that the needed priority must then be a good Bible study that's the envy of the city—notebooks, visuals, homework—the whole thing. However, in his research and preparation one day, he reads a pastoral peer's comment saying that, "The fact beats ceaselessly into my brain these days that there is a world of difference between knowing the Word of God and knowing the God of the Word."[34]

Missions

When Bible study doesn't revitalize his church, many pastors turn to a missions emphasis. Immediate efforts are made to become more fully involved in the outreach ministry of the church, both at home and on foreign soil. "A good missions program will build any church," he has been told. Again the leader is challenged by his peer: "The primary task of the Church is to worship God. Even the obvious evangelistic and missionary work must not take priority. God's people are called to be a worshiping community."[35] In his book, *Why Revival Tarries*, Leonard Ravenhill said: "The primary qualification for a missionary is not love for souls, as we so often hear, but love for Christ."

Community

"Community"—there is the keyword. The church leader grabs it and a whirl of social activity follows. "Our people are getting to know one another and the warmth of our love has made our evangelism more palatable,"[36] he reasons. Once again he is confronted with the challenge that:

> Evangelical or social activities can never be a substitute for this worship. If we neglect our foremost calling, we become spiritually arid in ourselves. We have nothing of lasting value to offer the world, and we dishonor God.[37]

Warfare

When work, Bible study, missions, and emphasis on the community fail to bring spiritual vitality to his congregation, the church leader is pressed in his spirit. Frustrated and oppressed, he reasons he must be under spiritual attack. Militancy becomes the new key word. The church must marshal its faith! "Rebuke, shield of faith, fiery darts, helmets and sword drills, and confession" become often repeated words and phrases. Deliverance becomes the rallying cry. Then again, while seeking new ammunition for his holy war against the forces of hell, he reads:

> Worship terrorizes the enemy of our souls, delights the heart of God, delivers mankind from bondage and transports us into the unsurpassed experience of the touch of heaven's hand upon a mortal soul. All, as nuggets in some vast gold mine, are hidden in the secret, worship![38]

When he sees his exhausted, wounded, and frustrated congregation constantly "binding" an enemy Christ said was defeated, the pastor realizes that instead of increased spiritual life, he is losing ground rapidly. His church has become a hospital for the wounded or an R&R facility for the weary. It is time to change the warfare presentation.

Prayer Meeting

"The return of the PRAYER MEETING is a MUST," shouts the preacher at the next service. A chorus of "amens" underscore his pronouncement. "We will all find a place to PRAY," he urges. Even though just a few people respond, he feels that this is the correct emphasis. The joy of "prioritizing" the important ministries of the church is, however, again questioned when he reads:

> Broadly speaking, prayer is the occupation of the soul with its needs. Praise is the occupation of the soul with its blessings. Worship is the occupation of the soul with God Himself.[39]

After wearing out both himself and his congregation with these attempts to revitalize the spiritual tone of the church, some Christian leaders are beginning to see that: "Worship is man's highest end, for it is the employment of his highest faculties in the sublimest object."[40] Any other first priority only moves the church into frustration and subsequent confusion. "All other wants are superficial and transient. The profoundest of all is the want of God. Let us rejoice then in His house. Heaven has no higher joy, the universe no higher work, than worship."[41] Andrew Murray agrees and writes: "To be alone in secret with the Father. This be your highest joy."[42] This "aloneness with the Father," however, takes its delight in corporate expression. The "highest joy" finds equal delight in ministering to the Lord in corporate expression when the whole body is come together.

Where Does Worship Originate?

We can know God only as He chooses to reveal Himself to us, and we need to come into His presence to receive greater revelation of Himself. Our progressive and growing response in worship is directly linked to the progressive illumination we are given of God's person, for we cannot worship God any higher than our concepts of Him. We respond in worship to One who has made Himself known to us, has spoken by His chosen messengers and by His Son, and has caused His Word to be written and shared with us. The writer to the Hebrews affirms the entirety of New Testament truth on this progressive revelation: "*God, who at sundry times and in divers manners spoke in time past unto the fathers by the prophets, hath in these last days spoken unto us by His Son.*"[43]

God speaks to us by His Son. God had to come to man before man could go to Him. Infinitely exalted and higher than our highest concepts, God reigns. Only through a voluntary disclosure on God's part, can His ways and thoughts be made known to His creation. Only by the permissive will of God, can man know His person.

"Acceptable worship, then, must take its character from the nature of God."[44] We must never forget that worship in the Spirit must come from God Himself. Andrew Murray closes Chapter 3 of his book, *With Christ in the School of Prayer*, with the prayer: "Teach me that the worship in spirit and truth is not of man, but only comes from Thee; that it is not only a thing of times and seasons, but the outflowing of a life in Thee."[45]

Worship begins with God. It is brought forth through a spiritual nature (Ephesians 2:10) and by the influence of the Spirit of God (Romans 8:13, 26; Ephesians 6:18). Worship is the acknowledgment of the worthiness of God (Revelation 4:11). He is worthy because His merciful kindness endures forever (Isaiah 54:8). He is the One Who alone is good (John 10:11). He is love even when hated of men (Jeremiah 31:3). He is righteousness even when man is unjust and full of malice (Psalm 112:3, 9). His exalted person is worthy to be worshiped in sincerity from the heart (Romans 1:9; Proverbs 23:26; Exodus 25:7; Psalm 119:108). This is the salt that seasons every sacrifice, and without the heart, worship "is a stage play."[46]

The Bible portrays God as worthy of our worship by virtue of His person. In the New Testament, the Apostle Paul speaks of Christ as the light which shown out of darkness (2 Corinthians 4:6). Peter epitomized the life and work of Jesus as one Who went about doing good (Acts 10:38). The book of Revelation is filled with descriptions of worship, both on earth and in heaven where the elders and creatures before the throne of God are portrayed as worshiping the Lamb. We hear them say, "*Worthy art Thou to take the scroll and to open its seals.*"[47] God is here worshiped for who He is, not for what He does for the worshiper.

It is understood then that both Old and New Testament worship is given by man to God primarily for who He is. Worship, however it is expressed, must be God centered. The thought and intent, the intense desire of the worshiper must be fixed upon God and not upon self or the concerns of self for blessings. Jeremiah, under the anointing of the Spirit, speaks the words of God to affirm God's desire: "*And ye shall seek me, and find me, when ye shall search for me with all your heart. And I will be found of you, saith the LORD: . . .*" [48]

How Is Worship to Be Expressed?

Christ by-passes the formalities of the Old Testament when speaking to the Samaritan woman at the well. He simplified the method of worship by saying, "*But the hour cometh and now is when the true worshipers shall worship the Father in spirit and in truth*" (John 4:23). This is uniquely the most definitive guideline given to worship in the New Testament. True worship of God cannot be reduced to rules, formulae, or ritual. It is, as Jesus said, an action that flows from the inner spirit and expresses the truth of how we feel about God. Worship on some occasions is exuberant, loud, and filled with the exciting presence of God's person. It may be absolutely quiet on other occasions; filled with the awe and respect of His glory. Neither way is better, for our inner feelings need a variety of expressions to remain truthful. We don't shout at a funeral, nor do we often weep at a ball game. The mood of the moment chooses the method of expression. If we are worshiping "in truth," we should expect variety in our worship expressions.

Believer priests as individuals and as leaders of worship must avoid ruts. Worshiping today in the same manner that was done yesterday can be empty formality if it is not an honest expression of what is in the heart at the present time. Ceremony and form can rob worship of its spontaneity and sincerity.

In England many years ago, Matthew Henry commented on Christ's remarks to the woman at the well in John 4:23 by cautioning believers:

> Christians shall worship God, not in the ceremonial observances of the Mosiac institution, but in spiritual ordinances, consisting less in bodily exercise, and animated and invigorated more with divine power and energy. The way of worship which Christ has instituted is rational and intellectual, and refined from those external rights and ceremonies with which the Old Testament worship was both clouded and clogged. This is called true worship in opposition to that which was typical.[49]

As editor of *The Speakers Bible*, James Hastings further cautions against the dangers of becoming mechanical in worship. Commenting on John 4:23, he concludes:

> The longer we use the forms of religion, the greater is this danger. We grow familiar with the most solemn observances and offices of religion, and they may end in becoming a soulless routine. We keep up the empty forms when the spiritual virtue is gone out of them. Only by ceaseless vigilance can we keep our religious observances fresh and make them real aids to the spiritual life. While therefore the due ordering and arrangement of them should be the subject of the most reverent thought and care, while our aim should be to make them the best possible of their kind, the most impressive and inspiring to the hearts of the worshipers, none the less they must ever hold a subordinate place and be used as means to a spiritual end.[50]

The "ceaseless vigilance" spoken of in the above quote must encompass care against mere performance. It is all too easy to fall into a performing leadership that directs rather than involves the church in worship. William Steuart McBirnie in his book, *The Search for the Early Church*, comments on the fallacy of a "performing" clergy before the audience of the laity by adding: "In the final sense, the audience of a worship service is not the congregation, but God.[51]

Corporate Expression

While worship is a very personal experience, worship in its most glorious form is the expression of the community of believers together. The steady process of individuals becoming "*built up a spiritual house*" (1 Peter 2:5) requires not only wise and involved leadership, but a willingness on the part of the ecclesia to become an involved community together. It requires a committed discipline to become a worshiping corporate body. It becomes necessary for all to work out their grievances so that a unity of love will allow for the greater flow of praise and worship. Uniquely, those offering worship receive the benefits of change in their own character while focusing on the throne and loving God corporately. It is "*beholding Him*" that "*we are transformed into His likeness with ever increasing glory*" (2 Corinthians 3:18, NIV). While each individual member must set his aim in the worship service, the entire body will find edification a result of released worship.

Oscar Cullman in his work, *Early Christian Worship*, says:

> We must assert here and now that the services of worship in the Protestant churches of our own era are very much poorer not only in respect of the free working of the Spirit, but also in respect of what is liturgical and especially in respect of what is aimed at in the gatherings of the community. The aim is constantly described by Paul as building up in the community (1 Corinthians 14).[52]

Cullman's book doesn't project worship's "aim" as being the edification of the Church, but rather edification as a result of God consciousness that comes through proper worship.

We are reminded in Psalm 149:4 that: "*The Lord taketh pleasure in His people.*" Somewhere along the line, the Church has forgotten that this is what gives pleasure to God. We are the object of His joy and our praise is the satisfaction of His own heart.

Do you see why we say that becoming a useful believer priest is an enterprise? We are engaged in a project or undertaking that is difficult, complicated, or risky, and there must be a readiness to engage in daring action. Experience shows that not all believers meet the eligibility requirements for this priestly assignment.

Chapter 2 Endnotes

1. 1 John 3:2

2. Revelation 1:6

3. Ephesians 1:12, NIV

4. Richard Francis Weymouth, *The New Testament in Modern Speech*, Boston, MA, The Pilgrim Progress, 1943

5. Ronald Knox, *The New Testament in the Translation of Monsignor Ronald Know*, NY, Sheed and Ward, 1944

6. *The Twentieth Century New Testament*, Chicago, IL, Moody Bible Institute

7. W*ebster's Seventh New Collegiate Dictionary*, A Merriam-Webster. C. & C. Merriam Company, Springfield, MA

8. Hebrews 7:25

9. Robert Webber, *Agenda for the Church: 1976-2000*, Eternity (1976) pp. 15-16. Paul E. Engle, *Discovering the Fullness of Worship*, (Philadelphia, PA, Great Commission Publications, 1978) pp.7-8.

10. Ibid

11. Ibid

12. Joseph S. Exell, editor, *The Biblical Illustrator*, Grand Rapids, MI, Baker Book House, 1968

13. Judson Cornwall, *New Wine Magazine*, December 1972, November 1976

14. Roxanne Brant, *Ministering to the Lord*, Florida, Roxanne Brant Crusades, 1973

15. *Webster's Seventh New Collegiate Dictionary*, A Merriam-Webster. C. & C. Merriam Company, Springfield, MA

16. Alfred P. Gibbs, *Worship, The Christian's Highest Occupation*, IA, Walterick Printing Co., 1953

17. David Bloomgren, *Scriptural Modes of Worship*, Portland, OR, 1978. The opinion expressed by David Bloomgren, Minister of Music at Bible Temple, Portland, Oregon. The address is on file on tape in the college library.

18. Judson Cornwall, *Let Us Worship*, p. 59, Bridge-Logos, NJ

19. Wesley Daniel Taylor, *Dancing With God; A Study in Contemporary Worship and Christian Action:* Ph.D. dissertation, School of Theology at Claremont, 1971. Note his work for the Doctor of Ministry Degree at Claremont School of theology: "It will be the purpose of this dissertation to strengthen the relationship between corporate worship and social action. Worship is self-centered and ingrown when it is not connected to the needs and problems of the world and its people."

20. See Genesis 27:20; I Samuel 25:23; II Samuel 14:33; 24:20.

21. See Genesis 24:52; II Chronicles 7:3; 29:29.

22. W. E. Vine, *An Expository Dictionary of New Testament Words*, Vol. IV, Set Z, (from prose—towards and Kueno—to kiss) NJ, Fleming H. Revell Co.,1966

23. Martin, Ralph P., *Worship in the Early Church*, London, Marshal, Morgan, and Scott, 1964

24. Psalm 89:3, 20

25. Romans 1:9; 12:1; 15:16

26. Leonard Ravenhill, *Why Revival Tarries*, pp. 1&21. MN, Bethany Fellowship, 1959

27. Matthew 13:22

28. Luke 21:34

29. Daniel 7:25

30. Leonard Ravenhill, *Why Revival Tarries*, p. 19. MN, Bethany Fellowship, 1959

31. Howard Moody, p. 94, 1969

32. Charles Finney, n.d., p. 57

33. Jay B. Oaks, *Rest Through Praise*, p. 102., New Hope Press, OH

34. Leonard Ravenhill,*Why Revival Tarries*, p. 59. MN, Bethany Fellowship, 1959

35. David Watson, *I Believe in the Church*, Grand Rapids, MI, Wm. B. Eerdmans 1978, p. 179

36. Howard Snyder, *The Community of the King*, IL, Inter-Varsity Press, 1978, Gene A. Getz, in *Sharpening the Focus of the Church*, Chicago, Moody Press, 1974; espouses this principle, also.

37. Richard Francis Watson, *The New Testament in Modern Speech*, Boston, MA, The Pilgrim Progress, 1943

38. Maureen Gaglardi, *The Key of David*, Canada, New West Press, 1966. An excellent example of this principle is given in Judson Cornwall's book, *Let Us Praise*, Bridge-Logos, NJ, 1973, pp. 71-73.

39. Gibbs, Alfred P., *Worship, the Christian's Highest Occupation*, IA, Walterick Printing Co., 1953

40. Joseph S. Exell, ed., *The Biblical Illustrator*, p. 355, Grand Rapids, MI. Baker Book House, 1968

41. Ibid., p. 356.

42. Andrew Murray, *With Christ in the School of Prayer*, p. 26, NJ, Fleming H. Revell Co., 1953

43. Hebrews 1:1-2

44. Joseph S. Exell, ed., *The Biblical Illustrator*, p. 356, Grand Rapids, MI, Baker Book House, 1968

45. Andrew Murray, *With Christ in the School of Prayer*, p. 22, NJ, Fleming H. Revell Co., 1953

46. Joseph S. Exell, ed., *The Biblical Illustrator*, p. 358, Grand Rapids, MI, Baker Book House, 1968

47. Revelation 5:9

48. Jeremiah 29:13-14

49. Matthew Henry, *Matthew Henry's Commentary On the Whole Bible*, Vol. V, p. 906, NY, Fleming H. Revell Co., 1935

50. James Hastings, *The Speaker's Bible*, Vol. 1, p. 109, Grand Rapids, MI, Baker Book House, 1962

51. William Steuart McBirnie, *The Search for the Early Church*, Wheaton, IL, Tyndale House Publishers, 1978

52. Oscar Cullman, *Early Christian Worship*, p. 26., Philadelphia, PA, The Westminister Press, 1953

3
The Eligibility for Priesthood
The Priestly Preparation

As exciting as it is to realize that Jesus has called us to be believer priests unto the Most High God, and as important as it is to worship and bring others into pure worship of God, we have only been issued a call. There is no compulsion, nor is this service automatic. The invitation to priesthood must be accepted, embraced, and prepared for. Remember what Jesus warned—"*For many are called, but few are chosen.*"[1] We might better understand this verse if we could read it, ". . . few have chosen."

God does not choose His priests from a list of favorites, nor does He choose by a game of chance. Personality, musical ability, holiness, or station in life play no part in determining God's call to priesthood. God has offered priesthood to all believers, but the decision to serve is a choice of individual Christians.

God provides the office, but He does not force anyone to serve. Even in the Old Testament there were times when Levites preferred to stay on the farm rather than serve at the tabernacle. Their tribal relationship was not forfeited, but their service in the priesthood was abandoned. They opted to not serve as priests. So have many believers in today's generation.

As we've already seen, God progressively revealed the pattern of the priesthood from the first Adam through the last Adam—Jesus.[2] God gave His pattern for the priesthood to Moses in minute detail when Israel came out of Egyptian bondage and God instituted the Aaronic priesthood to serve the needs of this developing nation. It became a pattern of priesthood throughout the world.

The Levitical Pattern for Preparation

The Old Testament believers could draw near to God only through a substitutionary sacrifice made available through the mediacy of a priest. The priest brought the penitent to God through the sprinkled blood, and then brought God's grace and forgiveness to the repentant one through the means of liturgy and ritual. For hundreds of years, these ceremonies of the priesthood were the only visible means of approach to God that were available.

After the coming of Christ, the Holy Spirit began to reveal that all the trappings of the Aaronic priesthood, including their vestments, ritual, and sacrifices, were but shadows of a reality that had come in Jesus Christ. Jesus told us, "*I am the way and the truth and the life. No one comes to the Father except through me.*"[3] We do not now come to God through ritual and sacrifice. Jesus is the exclusive channel to God's presence and grace. The book of Hebrews reveals the efficacy and the eternity of the high priestly office of Jesus—declaring that "*He is able to save completely those who come to God through him, because he always lives to intercede for them.*"[4] Jesus became the substance of which the Aaronic priesthood was but a shadow.

While Jesus did displace the Aaronic priesthood, He did so by fulfilling, not destroying, it. He testified, "*Do not think that I have come to abolish the Law or the Prophets; I have not come to abolish them but to fulfill them.*"[5] This is the position He expects His believer priests to take. Just as Jesus met the spiritual requirements of the Old Testament priesthood, so must we. As Paul put it, "*All these things happened to them as examples—as object lessons to us . . . they were written down so that we could read about them and learn from them in these last days as the world nears its end*" (1 Corinthians 10:11, TLB). While Paul's immediate subject was the sinning of Israel, his statement, "*All these things*," indicate the principles of that priesthood are still applicable to today's believer priests.

We rely heavily on the priesthood God established for Israel in the wilderness for understanding the principles of priesthood. God gave unequivocal direction as to who may serve, what was required of them, and how they were to perform their service. Nothing in the New Testament violates the spiritual principles behind these explicit directions.

One of the first spiritual principles to be seen in the Aaronic and Levitical priesthood was that the priests were prepared for their office. I see four obvious areas of preparation. First, they had to be born into the right family, for only members of the tribe of Levi could serve in the priesthood. Second, they had to be separated from the general encampment to live in tents pitched around the tabernacle. Third, they had to be properly trained. Fourth, their service was exclusively for God.

The New Testament Application of This Pattern Rightly Related

These same four areas of preparation are expected of believer priests. We need a correct birth. It is self-evident that we cannot serve as believer priests until we are believers. We must be born of the Spirit and made members of the household of faith, for only sons of God can serve as priests of God. It is not merely sad, it is tragic when individuals choose the priesthood, go to college and seminary to train for it, but have not been born again. It is like a member of the tribe of Gad trying to force his way into the priesthood when only members of the tribe of Levi could be selected. Worshipers must start at the cross—not at the college.

This son relationship with God must be kept viable for us to serve as His priests. Although our initial salvation will not be taken from us, we are clearly taught, "*Your iniquities have separated you from your God; your sins have hidden his face from you, so that he will not hear*."[7] How could we do the service of a believer priest if sin has so separated us from God that He cannot or will not hear us? There is a continuous need for the work of the cross in the life of a priest, for until his or her sins have been cleansed by the blood of Jesus, it is impossible to effect the cleansing of others. We have been promised:

> *His divine power has given us everything we need for life and godliness through our knowledge of him who called us by his own glory and goodness. Through these he has given us his very great and precious promises, so that through them you may participate in the divine nature and escape the corruption in the world caused by evil desires.*[8]

First we consistently remain partakers of His divine nature, then we can share that nature with others at the altar of worship.

Significantly Separated

Believer priests also have a call to separation, much as the entire tribe of Levi was moved from Israel's encampment and placed around the curtained fence that enclosed the tabernacle in the wilderness. They were both called out of the general camp and into the secluded priestly encampment. They were separated for service. Since much of their ministry was unto God, it was fitting that they live in close proximity to God's presence.

This is not a call for believer priests to cloister into Christian communities, for then there would be no spiritual light left in the world. What God wants from us is be separated from the world unto Himself. We may be with unbelievers in the business world or on an assembly line, but we are in fellowship with God in our spirit.

The call is still, "*Come out from among them and be separate, says the Lord. Touch no unclean thing, and I will receive you.*"[9] In His high priestly prayer, Jesus told His Father: "*These are in the world . . . They are not of the world, even as I am not of the world.*"[10] We are in the world, but not a part of it. We have been "*called . . . out of darkness into his marvellous light.*"[11] Our citizenship is in Heaven. We minister to and represent God here, but this is not our home. Paul called us "*Ambassadors.*"[12] We serve God here in the world system; we do not serve the world system if we are believer priests. This separation is essential to our priesthood. We have an avocation that pays the bills, but our vocation is priest unto God.

Spiritually Taught

Third, we must be taught to be believer priests. Perhaps the desire to worship is inherent in believers, but knowing how to worship acceptably is a learned experience. Just as the Levites encountered a lengthy training season before functioning as priests, so New Testament believers need to be trained to function as priests. We may be rightly born and completely separated, but if we don't know what we are doing, we are worthless as believer priests. Worship is more than standing and singing. Therefore, functioning as a believer priest and a worshiper requires more than a microphone, a guitar, and a keyboard. There is a need for a knowledge of holy things, means of approach to God, and what is an acceptable sacrifice to God.

It is interesting that the Levitical training involved the personhood of the priest—his living and relating to others, as well as his functioning in the priestly office. **Who they were** was as important to God as **what they did**. It still is. The life of the believer colors the ministry of the believer. It always has; it always will. We cannot function higher in Christian service than we are living in our relationship with God. In mere religious service, we can do one thing and live another, but in spiritual service our lives are on display, not our offices or personalities. Believer priests are dealing with the reality of Christ, not the ritual of religion. The purpose of this book that you are reading is to teach and train us to be effective believer priests.

A Divine Monopoly in Worship

Fourth, believer priests must embrace the exclusivity of their worship service. We must learn that what Jesus told Satan in the hour of temptation is still true: "*You shall worship the LORD your God, and HIM ONLY you shall serve.*"[13] God demands a monopoly on our worship. In His jealousy, He will not share worship with anything or anyone.

It is this fourth area of preparation for priestly ministry that forms the hub of this chapter. Just as the Old Testament priest was singly in Jehovah's service, we need to worship God exclusively. Our hearts need to be completely weaned from the idol gods of this world and focused restrictively on the true and living God.

The Hebrew children came out of more than 300 years of servitude to an extremely idolatrous nation. The Egyptians had hundreds of gods. These former slaves had been pressed into building temples for many of these deities, while they themselves had no place to worship Jehovah. It is not too amazing, then, that many of the Hebrews became worshipers of idols.

Their propensity for idolatry is mirrored in their insistence that Aaron build a golden calf as an object of worship during the time when Moses was on the mountain receiving the commandments from God. Their eager sacrifice of their newly acquired jewelry to provide the gold that was needed, and their wholehearted enthusiasm in their worship of the calf, heated God's anger to the point that He threatened to destroy the entire nation and start over with Moses. Moses interceded with God and called for volunteers to slay persons openly practicing this idolatry. Members of the tribe of Levi slew 3,000 idolaters that day with the sword. Read the entire story for yourself from Exodus, Chapter 32. It is a dramatic demonstration of how jealous God is in the matter of our worship.

God's choice of this tribe of Levi to serve as priests for the nation may well have been based on their wholehearted response to help Moses destroy this idolatry. One of the priestly responsibilities throughout Israel's history was to keep the people out of idolatry and locked into exclusive worship of Jehovah. They did well while Israel was becoming a nation, but the prophetic books declare that idolatry became rampant among these Hebrews after they became a strong nation.

Unfortunately, the Levite priests often joined the people in their idolatrous worship. God laments through the prophet Ezekiel:

> *The Levites that are gone away far from me, when Israel went astray, which went astray away from me after their idols; they shall even bear their iniquity . . . Because they ministered unto them before their idols, and caused the house of Israel to fall into iniquity; therefore have I lifted up mine hand against them, saith the Lord GOD, and they shall bear their iniquity.*[14]

Rather than leading the people to worship God, the priests allowed the people to press them into ministering unto idols. Ezekiel saw, in vision form, that this idolatrous worship was being done right in the Temple—God's house.

It is never easy to stand against the desires of people, but believer priests must take their orders from God, not from the congregation. It may be that the priests felt a strong stand for the worship of Jehovah would cost them their position with its security, but going along with the desire of the people cost them their relationship with God and incurred His wrath. It always will. Priests are not employees of the people they serve; they are servants of God.

Heart Preparation

To maintain purity of worship requires purity of heart. In the press of life, even the religious life, it is easy for our minds to become polluted and defiled. We often embrace popular concepts and philosophies without checking them against the Word of God. It is always easier to go with the crowd than to stand against it. Still, God's ways are not always the popular ideology of our generation, but His ways have stood the test of time, and they are not amendable by us.

In a time of national crises with the Philistines poised to attack Israel, Samuel, the second greatest man in Hebrew history, exceeded only by Moses, used his position as national priest to call Israel to a change of heart. We read:

> *And Samuel said to the whole house of Israel, "If you are returning to the LORD with all your hearts, then rid yourselves of the foreign gods and the Ashtoreths and commit yourselves to the LORD and serve him only, and he will deliver you out of the hand of the Philistines."*[15]

The Hebrew word here translated "serve" is *abad*: a worshiper, or a bond-servant. Samuel pled for Israel to cease worshiping the foreign gods and return to exclusive worship of Jehovah.

Samuel did not suggest a series of civil enactments or a great military stratagem in this crisis. He urged a return to the pure worship of God. Many years ago a great theologian wrote:

> The civilized statesmen of today may laugh at this primitive model of government and write with sarcastic dash, "Superstition," on its wish but might they not learn a lesson from its success that political woes are often to be remedied by moral reform, not by the mocked contrition and place-seeking miscreants but by the devout penitence of quiet stricken spirits.[16]

It is likely that the idols Samuel referred to were the Philistine gods. Most of the names of the Philistine gods were borrowed from the Canaanites whose principle god was El. The other chief deities of the Philistines were Dagon, Baal, Ashtoreth, and Beelzebub. Each of these gods represents a philosophy that through the years has cycled through the Church. Look at these last four mentioned names as an illustration of this truth.

Dagon—the God of Provision

It is curiously common to associate Dagon as half fish and half man. The association of Dagon with a fish goes back at least as early as Jerome (Circa A.D. 400), and the conception of the god as half fish goes back to David Kimshi (Circa A.D. 1200) both reflecting popular etymology, but the *Encyclopedia Britannica* declares that this concept is completely unsupported by any facts.

The name Dagon is almost certainly connected with the Semitic common noun for corn, or grain. Dagon was viewed as the god of vegetation during Abraham's time. The Philistines worshiped him as a god of provision. His help was employed when seeking a rich harvest.

The religious philosophy behind Dagon was that he was **a god of provision**. There are theologies afloat today that would teach us that the only practical reason to serve God is because He's got a Lincoln Continental in our tomorrow. It is wonderfully and scripturally true that God is a provisionary God Who provides our needs, but when a Dagon philosophy that God exists as the cosmic Santa Claus to bless us, that His whole reason for existence is simply to make provision for us, somewhere we've missed the heart of a divine sovereign God. If we hold tight to the hand of God because He is a provisionary God, we're going to miss the whole significance of worship altogether. Provision is a byproduct of our relationship with God; not the main product.

One wonders if the current prosperity doctrine in our churches may have its roots more in Dagon philosophy than the teaching of the Word of God. We cannot press into the heart of God if our whole thought during the course of prayer or praise is, "I know that as I do this, He's going to bless me with another goody tomorrow." When that is the ultimate driving force carrying us into prayer or praise, we have substituted the concept of Dagon for the revelation of Jehovah God, and God does not want to be seen as a New Testament Dagon. He's saying to us today through that ancient prophet of the Word, Samuel, that we put away this idol god from among us. This is a necessary part of heart preparation for believer priests. We dare not be priests offering worship to Dagon, the god of provision.

Baal—the God of Capriciousness

The second god of the Philistines was Baal. Baal is singular while Baalim is the plural form of the word. Baal was the most active of the Philistine gods. He was the son of Dagon. He was referred to as a dying and rising vegetation deity. Note how distinctly he is related to Dagon, the corn god or the god of provision.

Do you remember the story in 1 Kings 18:19-40 how Elijah challenged the prophet/priests of Baal on Mount Carmel? The challenge was: "*Then you call on the name of your god, and I will call on the name of the LORD. The god who answers by fire—he is God.*"[17]

He let the priests of Baal be first to offer a sacrifice. The prophets of Baal danced wildly around their sacrifice, even cutting themselves with knives. Elijah taunted them saying, "Well, maybe your god is sleeping, fellas, you know, maybe you ought to cry a little louder. Maybe he's away on a vacation and he'll hear you." With tongue in cheek, Elijah even dared to say: "Maybe your god is on the potty somewhere. You've just got to shout him out." Elijah was merely responding to the Philistine concept of Baal that Israel had adopted—a god of capriciousness. He comes at whim. He does what he wills to do, but you can never depend on him.

If we frame in our minds a philosophy that our God is a God of capriciousness, that He does what He wants when He wants and there is not a blessed thing we can do about it, we will have a

Baal concept of our God, not a Bible concept. God in all of His great sovereignty does do what He pleases, but mercifully He makes Himself available to be entreated with and talked to. It is intercessory prayer that stimulates the divine muscle of God as He extends His hand on the face of the earth.

We are not just pawns on an eternal chess board. God has greater designs for His people than that. We are not serving a god of capriciousness. We are serving a God of incredible love and grace Who wants to reveal Himself to the heart that is true and perfect or maturing before Him. Part of our heart preparation, as believer priests, is to put away from us the idea that our God is capricious, that He functions on whim. He has revealed to us that he functions on promise in response to prayer.

How could we honestly consider God as undependable? If there's ever anyone in the universe that is systematic, it is the Almighty. When He created this universe, He was extremely systematic. This universe runs like clockwork. The meteorologists can predict the exact minute the sun will rise or set on any given day of the year in any geographic location, and oceanographers can tell us the timing of high and low tides for any ocean in the world years in advance.

Nothing in life is more dependable than God's creation, because a non-capricious God made it so. If God said it, that settles it. If God started it, He will complete it. He is not a God of caprice; He is a God of constancy. He declared through the prophet Malachi: "*I the LORD do not change.*"[18] As a matter of truth, God is the only unchangeable quotient in our lives. Everything else is changing so rapidly that we need to run to stand still.

Some persons seem to have a Baal concept of Jehovah. They declare that He said one thing yesterday, but today He seems to contradict Himself. Not so. On Sunday they believe God loves them, but by Tuesday they feel God hates them, or at least has forgotten about them. The Apostle James had a grasp on the consistency of God, for he wrote: "*Every good and perfect gift is from above, coming down from the Father of the heavenly lights, who does not change like shifting shadows.*"[19] Jehovah and Baal have nothing in common. We must put away this strange god of Baal—the god of capriciousness—to be prepared to worship Jehovah God as believer priests.

Ashtoreth—the Goddess of Sex and Fertility

Ashtoreth is the lone goddess of the four chief Philistine gods. Ashtoreth is the plural for Astarte, the Hebrew is vocalized as *boseth*, which means shame to indicate Hebrew contempt for her cult. Astarte was the spouse of Baal of Carmel. Astarte was identified with the Egyptian deity Isis and also with the Greco/ Roman deities of Aphrodite and Venus. She was known as the goddess of fertility and reproduction.

We are living in an age when sex has become a driving goddess. This is true throughout the civilized world. Almost all advertising for merchandise has some sexual connotation to it, and it works so well there is little chance that it will diminish in the near future. Every day in a thousand ways, the goddess Ashtoreth is paraded in front of us. How imperative it is for believer priests to heed the word of the prophet to put away the gods of the Philistines to prepare our heart to worship the Lord.

Gentlemen, if you love Jesus and aspire to accept God's call to be a believer priest, challenge yourself to make covenant with your eyes and say, "Lord I want you to help me as a man to not feed the chambers of my imagery with the mud that the world throws at me. I put away the Ashtoreth of my life. I don't want this fertility goddess—this sexual innuendo to be constantly riding through the chambers of my imagery. I want God to be glorified in everything I think and do."

Ladies, the world is also flaunting Ashtoreth before your face in every conceivable form. You know what I'm talking about. Soap operas on television and love stories in magazines and books all extol lust and perversion under the name of love. Because lust has replaced divine love in our marriages, Christian homes are breaking apart at an alarming rate. Perhaps both the men and women in our churches have been over stimulated by the false goddess—the idol—of Ashtoreth. Ladies, join the gentlemen in saying, "God, I will accept the word of the prophet and cast or put away from me the gods of the Philistines, including the goddess of sex. I will prepare my heart to be a true believer priest of God."

Beelzebub—the God Who Creates and Sustains Wounds

The fourth Philistine god in the days of Samuel was Beelzebub—called the prince of demons by Jesus in the New Testament.[20] Jesus fully identified him with Satan.[21] Beelzebub means "The lord of flies." What an apt title for demons, for flies are drawn to hurts, wounds, cuts, and unhealed flesh, and so are the demons.

We may hastily say that we would never bow before the prince of demons—the Lord of the flies, but remember that any time we allow hurt, wounded flesh, or wounded emotions to remain unhealed, we become a prime target for the flies of darkness. If Satan cannot tempt us to bow before Dagon, the god of provision; Baal, the god of capriciousness; or Ashtoreth, the sex goddess, he will look for open wounds or cause them, so Beelzebub will have an entrance to our lives. I don't think Satan cares how he gains entrance to our minds and emotions, just so he gets in.

We're living in a season when Beelzebub is fiercely attacking some churches—leaving torn flesh and bleeding wounds throughout the families and friends of the split congregations. A church that has gone through a definitive split knows the depths of such wounds. The smell of blood attracts flies as far away as the next county. Those of us who have traveled through Egypt and Africa can testify to how quickly flies are drawn to wounds. Perhaps you have seen this for yourself on television. Whenever you see pictures of persons with swarms of flies teeming around and attaching themselves to open wounds, always remember that this is a picture in the natural of what Beelzebub, the lord of the flies, likes to do in the spiritual realms.

Not all wounds are caused by the prince of demons, for we can create our own wounds by our negative reactions to those very same kinds of splits or the things that people say. Saints, keep the lid on. Control your tongue. Don't be guilty of creating your own wound by an adverse reaction, an overt statement, or an anxious attitude over what someone else does. Go to God and confess the thing to God. Get healed quickly. If you don't, there's going to be a whole lot of buzzing around your brain. Satan knows how to attack, and the lord of the flies will do everything he can to feed on raw flesh. He'll agitate that wound until it has putrefied and filled with stench. What was only a wound that would have healed itself becomes an open doorway to infection and disease that can force an amputation to prevent a further spread of the disease. It is equally possible that it can cause death. Satan need not use a gun to destroy us. His flies will do the work even if it is far slower. Satan is an eternal being who has lots of time. He can afford to wait while we die painfully and slowly.

When we find ourselves with open wounds, we need to cry out to God and say, "Lord, I will not sustain the bleeding wound—the hurt. I will go and confess this thing to somebody and get some intercessory prayer. I'm not going to let bitterness mount up in my heart. I'm not going to let this thing continue to profusely bleed. I want the healing of God in this area so that the Beelzebub of the prince of darkness will not be the one who constantly keeps me swatting flies."

It is not enough to set our hearts to seek God. We must first instruct our hearts to forsake the influence the gods of this world have exerted upon us. This is step one in preparing our hearts to seek God. It was said of King Jehoshaphat: "*Nevertheless there are good things found in thee, in that thou hast taken away the groves out of the land, and has prepared thine heart to seek God.*"[21] These "groves" were places set up in Israel for the worship of the very gods we have looked at. The removal of these places of idol worship was considered by God as heart preparation for worship. It always will!

Eligibility for priesthood always begins with separation unto God. The first step of that separation is "out of" or "away from." It is the abandoning of the life that had proceeded entrance into the priesthood. There are groves in each one of our lives that need to be torn down. There are influences of idol gods that need to be cleansed out of our lives. Until this is done, nothing else can be done to make us quality believer priests.

The most important separation, however, is not "out of" or "away from," but "into" and "unto." Just as the Levites forsook their place in Israel's camp to pitch their tents around the tabernacle, so we must "forsake" as the first step in the process of coming closer to God's presence. We can't be a priest by correspondence or through the Internet. We must be in His courts in order to offer sacrifices on His altars.

By the way, in the economics of worship, the believer priest builds the altar upon which he will offer acceptable worship.

Chapter 3 Endnotes

1. Matthew 22:14

2. 1 Corinthians 15:45

3. John 14:6, *NIV*

4. Hebrews 7:25, *NIV*

5. Matthew 5:17, *NIV*

6. 1 Corinthians 10:11, *TLB*

7. Isaiah 59:2, *NIV*

8. 2 Peter 1:3-4, *NIV*

9. 2 Corinthians 6:17, *NIV*

10. John 17:11,16

11. Peter 2:9, *NIV*

12. 2 Corinthians 5:20

13. Matthew 4:10, *NIV*, emphasis added

14. Ezekiel 44:10,12

15. 1 Samuel 7:3, *NIV*

16. *The Biblical Illustrator,* 1 Samuel, pp. 166-167, Grand Rapids, MI, Baker Book House, 1967

17.1 Kings 18:24, *NIV*

18. Malachi 3:6, *NIV*

19. James 1:17, *NIV*

20. See Matthew 10:23; 12:24; Mark 3:22; Luke 11:15, 18-19

21. See Matthew 12:26; Mark 3:23; Luke 11:18

4
The Equipment for the Priesthood
The Believer Priest's Altar

What is a priest without an altar? He may be properly sanctified to his office, have beautiful vestments, excellent training, sufficient separation from false gods, and even have sacrifices to offer, but he cannot function without an altar. The altar was at the very heart of an Old Testament priest's service—both unto God and unto the people. It must have been instituted by God Himself, for both sons of Adam, Cain and Abel, understood the need of an altar and how it was to be used.

Perhaps it was unintentional or a subconscious act, but many Christian leaders have led persons to believe they must be in the church on Sunday to really touch God. They call the church building a "sanctuary of God"—a meeting place with God. Poetically this may be true, but in essence, the New Testament teaches that believer priests are the temple of God. Paul said:

> *Don't you know that you yourselves are God's temple and that God's Spirit lives in you?[1] If anyone destroys God's temple, God will destroy him; for God's temple is sacred, and you are that temple.[2] Do you not know that your body is a temple of the Holy Spirit, who is in you, whom you have received from God? You are not your own?[3] For we are the temple of the living God. As God has said: "I will live with them and walk among them, and I will be their God, and they will be my people.[4]*

This is not, of course, a release from public worship, for we are warned, "*Let us not give up meeting together, as some are in the habit of doing, but let us encourage one another—and all the more as you see the Day approaching.*"[5] The church building is where the believers meet; it is not the dwelling place of God. God does not dwell in man-made structures; He dwells in the lives of the redeemed.

Since believers are both individually and collectively the place where the Spirit of God resides as representative of the entire God-head, any divine altars will be in the hearts of those believers, not in the ornate, carved altars in cathedrals and stately church buildings. Church structures may be convenient and comfortable places to worship, but they are not the essential piece of equipment a believer priest must possess. An altar is the prime equipment needed.

Perhaps we get a hint of the personalization of altars in the plan God gave to Moses for the tabernacle in the wilderness. The largest piece of furniture was the Brazen Altar in the outer court. It was at this altar that all sacrifices were made. Although it was large enough to hold all other pieces of the tabernacle furniture,

God designed it so that it could be dismantled and carried from place to place when the cloud moved Israel to new camp sites. God's original design was a portable altar! Even the Golden Altar of incense in the Holy Place was portable. God didn't want His people to have to travel to find an altar. He placed an altar in the very midst of every camp that was ever pitched.

In the many special conventions and conferences on worship that have sprung up the past few years, we may have gained an impression that we need a keyboard, a guitar, a sound system and microphone, a sound track, and maybe even costumed dancers to be able to release worship to God. Fortunately, for many of us, the Bible keeps it far simpler than that. All we need in order to function as believer priests in the act of worship is an altar to God.

Altars Must Be Built

Although God designed the altar for the Old Testament tabernacle, it had to be constructed by the people. Every movement from campsite to campsite required the Levite priest to dismantle it, place it on carts, and reassemble it at God's chosen destination. God does not build altars. He instructs us to build our own altar.

Before the exodus from Egypt and the provision of the tabernacle, when men wanted to seek God, they built altars wherever they were. They had no specified place where worship was to be offered to God. The concept of a "holy city" and a "holy temple" came much later. Even much later, the New Testament declares that believers are both the "holy city" and the "holy temple." We, individually and collectively, are acceptable places to erect an altar, for the God we wish to worship dwells in us by His Holy Spirit.

This liberty to worship God in our soul and spirit means that we cannot worship at another's altar. Worship is an individual action. It is a believer responding to his or her God in a loving, submissive way. It really is quite a private action. Your altar probably will not work for me; I need my own altar.

It is obvious that the patriarchs built their own altars. Abraham built a new altar everywhere he went. So should we. We need not return to former places of worship; we can build an altar right where we are spiritually, emotionally, and physically.

Four materials were used in the construction of altars in the Old Testament: gold, brass, earth, and stones. The gold and brass (actually bronze) were used in the tabernacle. The golden altar was very small and was available to the priests only. It sat directly in front of the veil that separated the Holy Place from the Most Holy Place. No blood was offered on this altar; it was designed exclusively for the burning of incense. It was a place of worship unto God, and it was tended at least twice a day—morning and night. No individual could build a copy of this altar, and anyone found compounding incense to God's formulae to burn on any altar was sentenced to death.

The Brazen Altar was a place of God's judgment on sin. It was a place of death. It was where the sacrificial blood was sprinkled and the sacrifice burned. It is a severe type of Christ on Calvary's Cross taking all of God's judgment against sin upon Himself. We can merely identify with this altar; we cannot build one for ourselves. It was God's altar provided for mankind.

Altars of Earth

The materials God offered to individuals who wanted to build an altar unto God was earth and stones. He instructed them:

> *Make an altar of earth for me and sacrifice on it your burnt offerings and fellowship offerings, your sheep and goats and your cattle. Wherever I cause my name to be honored, I will come to you and bless you.*[6]

What could be simpler? Dirt of the earth was available everywhere. They did not need to import altar material, for it was under foot. They did not need divine materials. God is pleased with the materials we are familiar with, for, after all, God had used earth—soil—dirt—to form man.

Believer priests need to learn to take what is available to them and form it into an altar. It may not look like much, but if it becomes a place to touch God, it is holy—not intrinsically, but functionally. The home, the job, and the school room all contain enough earthiness to be pushed into a pile and made into a place to seek God.

As a pastor/counselor I have often had troubled persons tell me, "I feel dirty. My whole life is dirty." Do you sometimes feel that way? Why not use that dirt to form an altar where you can communicate with God? He is far less interested in the altar than He is concerned with what you have placed on that altar. Even the dirt of life can be used to form an altar unto God.

Altars of Stone

Altars of earth were usually one-time or temporary altars. Wind and rain would soon erode them away, so God also provided for constructing a more durable altar by using stones. He told them, "*If you make an altar of stones for me, do not build it with dressed stones, for you will defile it if you use a tool on it.*"[7]

Once again God instructed them to build altars of common, available materials. All who have visited Israel and the surrounding territories will corroborate the great availability of stones. It seemed that God wanted them to use what was readily available to them for constructing a place to contact Him. No imports are necessary. Use what is at hand.

As a pastor I tried earnestly to break the habit of people trying to use King James English when praying to God. It is awkward, unnatural, and frequently fails to express the true inward desires of the individual. That was the common, everyday English of people at the time the King James Bible was translated, but no one uses such language in everyday conversation any more. Why not use what is available? Children should pray like children. I am not impressed when they talk to God like adults, unless that is the way they talk to me later. I've learned through the years that persons with multiple languages are usually more comfortable using their mother tongue in prayer. Why not? That's the natural rock of their lives.

In insisting that the stones not be changed in shape, I think God was saying for us to be natural when we approach Him. Don't try to fancy things up for His sake. He knows the real us. He died for us when we were bigger messes than we are now. "Come just as you are" is the title of an old hymn we may need to start singing again.

"*Make an altar of stones for me.*" What is a stone? Just a rock. A hard thing. Don't our lives have plenty of hard things in them? We can curse them, bury them, decorate them, throw them, or we can build an altar unto God out of them.

Where do stones come from? The geologists tell us that there are only three basic types of stones on the face of the earth: igneous rock, metamorphic rock, and sedimentary rock. Each is formed differently.

Igneous rock comes from deep within the earth where molten or melted magma exists. When a volcano erupts, it spews this magma out and we call it lava. It was formed in the fire and spewed out on the surface of the earth through great violence. Most of us have lava rock on the surface of our lives. A deep inner fire of anger, fear, or hurt has melted molten magma that may have burned in our soul for years until something triggered an eruption that spewed it onto the surface of our lives. When it cooled, it left porous lava rock all over us. What shall we do with these cold evidences of past eruptions? Build an altar! God will accept worship on an altar of igneous rocks.

The *metamorphic rock* is a product of a deep pressure under the earth. The chemical actions of liquids and gases combined to bring together the elements that form metamorphic rock. Marble is a good example of this kind of rock. No pressure; no marble!

All of us have experienced inner pressure. At times we thought it would destroy us. We cried out to God for relief from the pressure, but instead of removing that pressure, He used it to form beautiful marble in our inner being. It is an excellent construction material. Use it to build an altar unto God.

What is called *sedimentary rock* is a product of extreme temperature change and consists of materials that once were part of older rocks. Sandstone is an example of sedimentary rock. There is no waste in God's program. God can, by the work of His Spirit, use bits and pieces of other stones that we felt were worthless and "recycle" them into beautiful sandstone. We can take this rock and form it into an altar.

We don't need heavenly materials from which to construct our altars as believer priests. We all have sufficient rocks in our lives to form an altar unto God. Some were formed by an inner fire, some by great pressure, and others by extreme temperature changes—we've gone from hot to cold over and over again in our walk with God. We need merely gather and stack these stones into a rudimentary form that will hold the sacrifice of our lips and lives.

There was, however, one prohibition in building an altar of stones. God clearly said, "*If you make an altar of stones for me, do not build it with dressed stones, for you will defile it if you use a tool on it.*"[8] They were not allowed to change the shape of the rocks. It is possible that God is warning believer priests against changing the shape of the hard things in their lives. Don't reshape the story to make the hard thing look like someone else's fault. Don't try to make it look like a hard place you've seen in another's life. Don't try to diminish the size of the stone. Keep your stones natural! If God wanted uniformity, He would have required the altars to have been built with bricks. Instead, He asked for stones—each of which would be different than the others.

Francis Frangipane says:

> We will never know Christ's victory in its fulness until we stop reacting humanly to our circumstances. When you truly have authority over something you can look at that thing without worry, fear or anxiety. . . . Generally speaking, the essence of who we are is made of events and how we responded to those events . . . With few exceptions, those events which we remember the most have shaped us the most . . . although the events of our lives are irreversible, our reactions to those events can still be changed.[9]

We need not react against or seek to change the circumstances of our lives. Pick up those stones, no matter how they were formed, and build them into an altar where God can be contacted, worshiped, and glorified.

Altars Are for Cleansing the Priest

It is noteworthy that when God established the ministry of the altar for the tabernacle, the first persons to participate there were the priests. The first sacrifice was for the priests. The first blood was sprinkled by Moses on the house of Aaron. Until they were cleansed, consecrated, and anointed there could be no ministry to the house of Israel. Furthermore, the priests were instructed to daily eat portions of the sacrifices that were brought to be offered unto God. Paul asks, "*Consider the people of Israel: Do not those who eat the sacrifices participate in the altar?*"[10]

When the nation of Israel was strengthened and enlarged under David's reign, the priests served by courses. Between their tour of duty, they were free to go home and tend their farms or businesses. When it was time for them to resume their priestly duties, the first step was to go to the altar to offer another sacrifice to cleanse them from all defilement they may have accumulated during their time out of priestly service. Should it be any different for believer priests? God will not accept the ministry of a defiled priest, no matter how beautifully it is performed, but He can and will cleanse the defilement from the believer priest's life if we request it.

We rejoice in the truth that Christ offered a sacrifice for sin once and for all. Still, none of us lives completely without sin. The apostle John declares, "*If we claim we have not sinned, we make him out to be a liar and his word has no place in our lives.*"[11] Christ need not be sacrificed repeatedly, but we need to apply that sacrifice on a daily basis. We are not sinless ones; we are forgiven ones. Defiled thoughts, words, and deeds need to be brought again to Christ for His forgiveness and our cleansing. The altar where we make contact with Jesus and offer confession of sin and weakness is the altar we have built in our own hearts of the earth and stones in our lives. We need not find our way back to Calvary—we need but find our way to the Christ of Calvary at our heart altars.

Altars Are for Seeking God

Are you familiar with the story of Balaam? Numbers 22-24 tells the story in considerable detail. When Israel was in the wilderness, their presence became a threat to King Balak. He sent for a known prophet by the name of Balaam and offered him substantial financial reward if he would curse Israel. In spite of God's warning, Balaam journeyed to Balak to offer his services. Four times on four separate mountain peaks Balaam called for Balak to build an altar and offer seven oxen and seven rams.

> *Then Balaam said to Balak, "Stay here beside your offering while I go aside. Perhaps the LORD will come to meet with me. Whatever he reveals to me I will tell you." Then he went off to a barren height. God met with him, and Balaam said, "I have prepared seven altars, and on each altar I have offered a bull and a ram." The LORD put a message in Balaam's mouth and said, "Go back to Balak and give him this message."*[12]

The prophet was out of the will of God, but he was quite certain God would meet him if he would build altars and seek His face. Out of this most unusual encounter, came the glorious prophecy about the birth of Jesus: "*I see him, but not now; I behold him, but not near. A star will come out of Jacob; a scepter will rise out of Israel.*"[13]

Balaam was disobeying God and had a mercenary motivation, but he succeeded in contacting God through the altar. So can we, especially when we fervently seek God out of a pure heart.

The term *to seek*, as in seeking the Lord, is one of the strongest worship terms in the Bible. The Hebrew words we translate *to seek* focus the thrust on seeking God so as to find Him to love. It is not seeking Him to offer petition as much as to offer Him our love.

Two Hebrew words in our Bible are translated "to seek." *Strong's Concordance* defines the word *baqash* as "to seek in worship and prayer," and the word *darash* as "to diligently inquire; to worship." Al Novak translates this word "to find someone to love."[14]

These two words for seeking God are widely used in the Old Testament. Let's look at five examples. The superscript letters [a] or [b] will indicate which Hebrew word is translated "to seek." Letter [a] stands for *baqash*—"to seek in worship and prayer," while [b] signifies *darash*—"to diligently inquire; to worship." The first example comes from 1 Chronicles 22:19:

> *Now set your heart and your soul to seek*[b] *the Lord your God; arise therefore, and build ye the sanctuary of the Lord God, to bring the ark of the covenant of the Lord, and the holy vessels of God, into the house that is to be built in the name of the Lord.*

The people were challenged to focus their inner natures to worship until they found the object of their love—Jehovah. They needed "to find someone to love" since love motivation would be more than sufficient to challenge them to build a house for the Lord. There cannot be a higher motivation for service to the Lord than to fall in love with Him completely.

We see these two words again in Deuteronomy 4:29-31:

> *But if from thence thou shalt seek*[a] [if you begin to pray and worship] *the Lord thy God, thou shalt find him, if thou seek*[b] [if you are praying and worshiping to where your eyes are focused on Him alone. You're not seeking things, but just lost in the wonder of His majesty and earnestly desiring Him] *him with all thy heart and with all thy soul. When thou art in tribulation, and all these things are come upon thee, even in the latter days, if thou turn to the Lord thy God, and shalt be obedient unto his voice; (For the Lord thy God is a merciful God;) he will not forsake thee, neither destroy thee, nor forget the covenant of thy fathers which he sware unto them.*

Note also 2 Chronicles 11:16:

> *And after them out of all the tribes of Israel such as set their hearts to seek*[a] *the Lord God of Israel came to Jerusalem, to sacrifice unto the Lord God of their fathers.*

Those who came to Jerusalem to *baquash*—to pray and worship—had their hearts set on finding God. Prayer and worship were not secondary to them; it was the primary channel through which they sought God. So should be our praise and worship. If it is an end in itself, it becomes a puny thing. All praise and worship should have finding God in a fresh way at its ultimate end.

A fourth example of the use of the Hebrew word *darash* in the books of history concerns the young King Hezekiah.

> *And in every work that he (Hezekiah) began in the service of the house of God, and in the law, and in the commandments, to seek*[b] *his God, he did it with all his heart, and prospered* (2 Chronicles 31:21) .

This young king earnestly sought God as the object of his love, and God not only revealed Himself to Hezekiah, He prospered him. The king sought God, not prosperity, and found both. Has God changed or have we?

Hezekiah sought and worshiped God in *darash* fashion. He diligently inquired—seeking to find that someone to love, and he did it with all his heart. He learned to focus himself while seeking. His mind did not wander onto other things as ours often do. We begin to praise and worship and then mentally go out to check the car or to wonder if the iron got turned off before we left the house. He had learned to: "*Gird up the loins of your mind*" (1 Peter 1:13). Nothing in his mind was flapping; everything was tied down for the task of seeking God in worship until there was a love flow between himself and his God.

We must also take a look at where, again, both Hebrew words for "seek" occur. In 1 Chronicles 16:10-11, we read: "*Glory in His holy name; Let all rejoice (samach*) who seek*[a] *the Lord. Seek*[b] *the Lord and his strength, seek*[a] *his face continually.*" (**Samach* = to make very glad.)

Something wonderful happened when these persons sought the Lord in joyful worship and prayer. Our altars are not only places of repentance; they are equally places for rejoicing. We do not seek to come into the presence of *the Judge of all the earth*,[15] we seek to come into the presence of our lover in repentance, intercession, worship, and rejoicing.

Interestingly enough, these channels of worship are all anointing levels that flow from the heart of God. Repentance is a gift of God and flows from God to man. Intercession is an anointing of God that flows from God through man to the object of concern. Each of these is a God-given tool to help us in our seeking God through worship at the altars we build.

Worship is an anointed release of God that flows from God through man and returns to God. Don't forget that long before we rejoice in God, He rejoices over us, for He said, "*The LORD your God is with you, he is mighty to save. He will take great delight in you, he will quiet you with his love, he will rejoice over you with singing.*"[16]

To rise to the ministry of the believer priest requires that our hearts seek His heart. It also requires us to be open to the searching of His heart as He investigates worshipers looking for someone who is worshiping "*in spirit and in truth.*"[17] God will reveal Himself to such a worshiper. It opens the door for great revelations of spiritual truths, and it unfolds a revelation of God to the individual who has searched diligently for Him. When that begins to happen, you have what we have historically called revival. Most of what we call "revival" are actually results of revival. Revival is when a person and His God meet face to face in loving relationship. This is more apt to happen at the altar than at the pulpit, for revival comes out of renewed relationships, not out of reheated sermons.

Altars Are for Prayer

From the days of Enosh, Adam's grandson, "*men began to call on the name of the LORD.*"[18] One characteristic we see in those who sought an audience with God was the building of an altar. They saw the altar as a place for remission of sins and a place for communication with God. So should we. The book of Hebrews reminds us, "*Seeing then that we have a great high priest, that is passed into the heavens . . . Let us therefore come boldly unto the throne of grace, that we may obtain mercy, and find grace to help in time of need.*"[19]

It seems that our altars and God's throne are inexorably connected. Christ's sacrifice has opened a door into heaven that guarantees that our prayers will be heard. John told the Church,

> *This is the confidence we have in approaching God: that if we ask anything according to his will, he hears us. And if we know that he hears us—whatever we ask—we know that we have what we asked of him.*[20]

We have a direct channel to heaven at the altar we build in our lives. It is a dedicated line to God's throne. From our position of worship, we talk to the Father as Jesus talked to His Father. We know He hears us, so we ask in assurance of faith. Some of this speaking is on our own behalf. We make our requests known and He grants them if it is in His will for us. Other times our prayer becomes intercession for the needs of others. We do not initiate this form of prayer. The Holy Spirit within us initiates it, but it is powerful in its results.

Andrew Murray, a most devout man of God, wrote,

> Christ meant prayer to be the great power by which His Church should do its work . . . the neglect of prayer is the great reason the Church lacks greater power over the masses in Christian and heathen countries.[21]

If we would use our altars as places of prayer, the Spirit within us would increasingly inspire us to pray His prayers in intercession for needs throughout the world.

There is, however, an even more beneficial aspect to prayers offered from personal altars, and that is learning to hear God speak to us. If prayer is communication with God, it should be a two way conversation. Far too many prayers are presented as a monologue, while God desires to have a dialog with us.

We need to pause and listen in prayer time. Perhaps the instruction the High Priest Eli gave to young Samuel would help us. He said to tell God, "*Speak, for your servant is listening.*"[22]

This unwillingness to listen to God speak is one of the major causes for unanswered prayer, for it becomes unheard prayer. Twice in the Old Testament God said:

> *Because I have called, and ye refused; I have stretched out my hand, and no man regarded; . . . Then shall they call upon me, but I will not answer; they shall seek me early, but they shall not find me:*[23] *'When I called, they did not listen; so when they called, I would not listen,' says the LORD Almighty.*[24]

It seems that God is less anxious to hear a lecture than He is to enter into a conversation with us. If we won't hear Him, He stops listening to us.

Remember that in the Scripture "to hear" is equivalent to our "to heed." We do what God says if we really hear Him, for as Samuel told King Saul, "*Does the LORD delight in burnt offerings and sacrifices as much as in obeying the voice of the LORD? To obey is better than sacrifice, and to heed is better than the fat of rams.*"[25]

Hearing God and heeding what He says is the route into a righteous life so necessary for the believer priest.

Chapter 4 Endnotes

1. 1 Corinthians 3:16, *NIV*
2. 1 Corinthians 3:17, *NIV*
3. 1 Corinthians 6:19, *NIV*
4. 2 Corinthians 6:16, *NIV*
5. Hebrews 10:25, *NIV*
6. Exodus 20:24, *NIV*
7. Exodus 20:25, *NIV*

8. Exodus 20:25, *NIV*

9. Francis Frangipane, *The Three Battlegrounds* p. 40, 70 River of Life Ministries, Marion, IA, 1989

10. 1 Corinthians 10:18, *NIV*

11. 1 John 1:10, *NIV*

12. Numbers 23:3-5, *NIV*

13. Numbers 24:17, *NIV*

14. *Hebrew Honey*, p. 230, Al Novak Heritage Printers and Publishers, Dallas, TX, 1987

15. John 4:24

16. Genesis 18:25, *NIV*

17. Zephaniah 3:17, *NIV*

18. Genesis 4:26, *NIV*

19. Hebrews 4:14, 16

20. 1 John 5:14-15, *NIV*

21. Andrew Murray, *The Ministry of Intercessory Prayer*, p.12, originally published in 1897 under the title, *The Ministry of Intercession,* Bethany House Publishers, Minneapolis, MN, 1981

22. 1 Samuel 3:10, *NIV*

23. Proverbs 1:24, 28

24. Zechariah 7:13, *NIV*

25. 1 Samuel 15:22, *NIV*

5
The Enablement of the Priesthood
The Believer Priest's Righteousness

Anyone can build an altar and offer some form of sacrifice on it. Cain and Abel, the sons of Adam, both built altars and offered sacrifices on them, but God accepted the sacrifice of Abel while utterly rejecting the sacrifice of Cain. We've already seen that while Abel offered the sacrifice of a lamb, which necessitated the shedding of blood, Cain offered vegetables and grain, for he was a farmer.

One son willingly offered what God had specified, but the other substituted what he wanted to give. Abel worshiped in divine righteousness, while Cain approached God in self-righteousness.

Perhaps he did not know what we have come to understand: "*All of us have become like one who is unclean, and **all our righteous acts are like filthy rags**; we all shrivel up like a leaf, and like the wind our sins sweep us away.*"[1]

Any exercise of self-will as a replacement for the revealed will of God is an act of unrighteousness, and the unrighteous cannot stand in God's presence to minister as priests. Paul asks, "*Know ye not that the unrighteous shall not inherit the kingdom of God?*"[2]

The standing of the person is as important as the sacrifice he brings. What we *are* always takes precedence over what we *do*. The personhood of the priest determines the acceptance or rejection of his sacrifice. We cannot worship God successfully out of an impure heart. Cain learned this the hard way.

The Need for Righteousness

It is entirely possible to build an altar and never use it. Some persons who are good at construction have never truly entered into the priesthood. This was true in the wilderness where the God appointed builders of the tabernacle were not the men who used it. God chose the tribe of Levi and the family of Aaron to serve as priests. These men were like the rest of the Hebrews who had come out of Egypt, but they had a special calling and consecration on their lives.

To help identify these men as divinely appointed priests, God provided special garments for them to wear. This set them apart from their brethren. It made identifying them easier for the worshipers who needed their services. In a sense, these priestly garments were uniforms with God's insignia on them much as police officers have identifying uniforms and badges.

These priestly garments also kept the priest focused on who he was and what was expected of him. If his mind began to wander back to the homestead, wife and children, he was brought back to his priesthood responsibilities by one glance at his robe. His calling was signified by his clothing.

God provided a work uniform that was worn when ministering in the outer court, but He furnished a special, and very ornate, robe for the High Priest to wear when he came into the presence of God in the Holy of Holies. This garment could never be worn in the outer court, for it did not signify separation from other persons; it spoke of separation unto God.

We are believer priests chosen by God for spiritual service and worship. When we function in our priestly ministries we, too, are to be clothed in special uniforms. The psalmist sang, "*May your priests be clothed with righteousness; may your saints sing for joy.*"[3]

Righteousness is the official uniform for New Testament believer priests. The prophet Isaiah realized this, for he said:

> *I delight greatly in the LORD; my soul rejoices in my God. For he has clothed me with garments of salvation and arrayed me in a robe of righteousness, as a bridegroom adorns his head like a priest, and as a bride adorns herself with her jewels.*[4]

Salvation is the inner garment; righteousness is the outer garment. The believer priest comfortably feels the garment of salvation, but those to whom and with whom he ministers, sees the outer garment of righteousness that God has provided.

Isaiah's allusion to the bride and bridegroom's ceremonial dress brings to mind Matthew's account of a parable Jesus told. In this story, Jesus said that a king sent his servants to gather guests for a royal wedding. Each guest was provided with a wedding garment. When the king came to greet the guests, he saw one man among them who wasn't wearing the garment.

> *"Friend," he asked, "how did you get in here without wedding clothes?" The man was speechless. Then the king told the attendants, "Tie him hand and foot, and throw him outside, into the darkness, where there will be weeping and gnashing of teeth." For many are invited, but few are chosen.*[5]

Proper garments are important to God. This person had been invited, had accepted the invitation and showed up, but he didn't wear the correct attire. It would have cost him nothing to wear it, for it was provided by the king. This refusal cost him dearly.

Is it not likely that far more persons have been chosen to be believer priests than are willing to take the time to be clothed with salvation and righteousness? "*For many are called, but few are chosen*" is an ongoing reality. God does not choose His believer priests by casting lots. He merely looks for those who are wearing His provided garments of salvation and righteousness.

God's priests may come from every tribe on the earth, and they may have found fellowship and training in diverse religious groups, denominations, or fellowships. If they are His priests, they have all been saved by the shed blood of Jesus Christ, and they all are clothed with the robes of God's righteousness. Like a choir of mixed races, their faces may be different, but their robes are all alike, which produces a visual uniformity.

The Nature of Righteousness

Please do not interchange the terms *righteousness* and *holiness*. Neither is a synonym for the other. Holiness has to do with being—what we are. Righteousness has to do with standing—what we do. Holiness is reflected in our character, while righteousness is reflected in our calling. Holiness is the essential nature of God being lived in us by the Holy Spirit, while righteousness is the way we live our Christian life in this world.

Righteousness, which is imputed by Christ and received by faith, leads to holiness—it is a pathway or part of the process of bringing holiness into our lives. The Word says: "*Just as you used to offer the parts of your body in slavery to impurity and to ever-increasing wickedness, so now offer them in slavery to* ***righteousness leading to holiness***."[6]

Right-standing before God puts us in a position to participate in His holiness. If we cannot stand in His presence, how can we expect to partake of His nature?

In speaking of righteousness, Lawrence O. Richards says:

> The underlying idea is one of conformity to a norm. People are righteous when their personal and interpersonal behavior accords with an established moral or ethical norm. In the Old Testament there is only one standard by which righteousness can be measured — the revealed will of God, particularly as it is expressed in the law. . . . Thus, the Old Testament does not deal primarily with abstract or absolute righteousness. When a person is said to be "righteous," no suggestion of sinlessness is implied. Instead, the statement implies actions in harmony with one's obligations in his or her relationship with God.[7]

Notice that Old Testament righteousness is identified as "conformity with God's will and order." God's word through Samuel to King Saul still applies: "*Does the LORD delight in burnt offerings and sacrifices as much as in obeying the voice of the LORD? To obey is better than sacrifice, and to heed is better than the fat of rams.*"[8]

Doing what God has said—the way He said to do it—is righteousness. No substitutions are acceptable. Among the things God instructed the Israelites to teach to their children was:"*If we are careful to obey all this law before the LORD our God, as he has commanded us,* ***that will be our righteousness****.*"[9]

Obedience to the Word of God is the basis of righteousness. Neither emotion nor good works can substitute for obedience in coming into righteousness in the Old Testament. This does not change in the New Testament, except that Christ becomes this conformity to God's will and order for us.

The word righteousness appears 306 times in 289 verses in our Bible, so it must be important to us for God to have spoken of it so often in the pages of His book. He makes it clear that He is righteous in all His ways, and that He expects righteousness in us as well. Fortunately for us, He makes His righteousness available to us as a gift, for Paul wrote:

> For if, by the trespass of the one man, death reigned through that one man, how much more will those who receive God's abundant provision of grace and of the **gift of righteousness** reign in life through the one man, Jesus Christ. [10]

The Provision of Righteousness

Remember, righteousness does not center itself around the holiness of a person's life. Righteousness deals with that person's "standing" or "position" before God. Standing in Christ means that I am standing before the Father's throne in the will and order of God. This "standing" or "position" before God is actualized by being in the will and order of God. The New Testament shows that "*Christ is . . . made unto us . . . righteousness.*"[11]

What a relief! What God has required of us, He has already given to us. Through generations of dealing with Israel, God verified man's inability to completely obey God. Many, such as Moses, made great strides in obeying God's rules and laws, but all failed in one or more of them. Disobedience in one decree disannulled the obedience in the others. It was all or nothing at all.

God could not rewrite His law, nor could He wink at sin. He required righteousness of all who would be identified with Him, but fallen human nature has consistently been incapable of dependable obedience to the will and ways of God. So:

> *What the law was powerless to do in that it was weakened by the sinful nature, God did by sending his own Son in the likeness of sinful man to be a sin offering. And so he condemned sin in sinful man, in order that the righteous requirements of the law might be fully met in us, who do not live according to the sinful nature but according to the Spirit.*[12]

Jesus came to completely fulfill the law of God. He testified: "*Do not think that I have come to abolish the Law or the Prophets; I have not come to abolish them but to fulfill them.*"[13]

Christ, the representative man, fulfilled every standard of righteousness given in the Old Testament, and that righteousness has been made available to us through impartation and imputation. Impartation is to project, transfer, or make known from one to another. Paul told the believers in Rome: "*I long to see you so that I may impart to you some spiritual gift to make you strong.*"[14]

Paul wanted to share something he had received from God with these Christians. He wanted to "impart" to them, to transfer from himself to them a spiritual gift or grace. It is similar to what he told the Corinthian believers:

> *For I received from the Lord what I also passed on to you: The Lord Jesus, on the night he was betrayed, took bread, and when he had given thanks, he broke it and said, "This is my body, which is for you; do this in remembrance of me.*"[15]

By revelation, Paul had received a spiritual understanding of what the Lord's Supper really meant, and he sought to confer, endow, implant, instill, share, transmit, or pass on that revelation. This is what impartation means.

This is what Christ does when He imparts His righteousness to us. He takes what He has received from His Father and imparts it to us. He is on record as having perfectly obeyed the law of God. Now he imparts that record to us. He endows us with His righteousness. He instills righteousness in us. He shares His complete obedience with us as an endowment.

The righteousness of Christ comes to us not only through impartation, but through imputation. By imputation we mean, as Webster's Dictionary says, "to set to the account of." It is similar to someone making a deposit to your bank account. Paul uses the example of Abraham to illustrate this truth. He writes:

> *Yet he* [Abraham] *did not waver through unbelief regarding the promise of God, but was strengthened in his faith and gave glory to God, being fully persuaded that God had power to do what he had promised. This is why "it was credited* [King James "imputed"] *to him as*

righteousness." The words "it was credited to him" were written not for him alone, but also for us, to whom God will credit righteousness—for us who believe in him who raised Jesus our Lord from the dead. [16]

Three things are credited to Abraham here: (1) He was strong in faith, (2) He gave glory to God, and (3) He was fully persuaded that God would do what He had promised. This is an excellent way to come into Christ's imputed righteousness.

Oswald Chambers reminds us that this imputation is not totally one sided—we have some responsibility in this. He wrote:

> No one is ever united with Jesus Christ until he is willing to relinquish not sin only, but his whole way of looking at things. To be born from above of the Spirit of God means that we must let go before we lay hold, and in the first stages it is the relinquishing of all pretense. What Our Lord wants us to present to Him is not goodness, nor honesty, nor endeavor, but real solid sin; that is all He can take from us. And what does He exchange for our sin? Real solid righteousness. But we must relinquish all pretense of being anything, all claim of being worthy of God's consideration.[17]

Theologians have long used the term "double imputation" to describe the work of the cross. By this they mean that we impute (impart, cast) our sins to Jesus, and He, in turn, imputes His righteousness to us. It seems that until we cast our sins upon the Cross, Christ cannot impart His righteousness to us.

Oswald Chambers reminds us that:

> Imputed righteousness must never be made to mean that God puts the robe of His righteousness over our moral wrong, like a snow-drift over a rubbish heap; that He pretends we are all right when we are not. The revelation is that "Christ Jesus is made unto us, righteousness;" it is the distinct impartation of the very life of Jesus on the ground of the Atonement, enabling

me to walk in the light as God is in the light, and as long as I remain in the light God sees only the perfections of His Son. We are "accepted in the Beloved.[18]

There is a beautiful example of this in the minor prophets. The visionary prophet, Zechariah, described his vision like this:

> *Then he showed me Joshua the high priest standing before the angel of the LORD, and Satan standing at his right side to accuse him. The LORD said to Satan, "The LORD rebuke you, Satan! The LORD, who has chosen Jerusalem, rebuke you! Is not this man a burning stick snatched from the fire?" Now Joshua was dressed in filthy clothes as he stood before the angel. The angel said to those who were standing before him, "Take off his filthy clothes." Then he said to Joshua, "See, I have taken away your sin, and I will put rich garments on you." Then I said, "Put a clean turban on his head." So they put a clean turban on his head and clothed him, while the angel of the LORD stood by.*[19]

Please remember that this is a vision; not a historical fact. Joshua, the son of Nun, was the assistant to Moses, and later became his replacement as leader of Israel. He was not of the tribe of Levi, and therefore was ineligible for the priesthood.

The Joshua who Zechariah saw was a representative priest; probably a high priest. He came into the presence of God to make atonement for the people, but Satan was there to challenge his right to stand before God. It was obvious to Zechariah in this vision that this Joshua was clothed in filthy garments. No high priest would dare to enter the Holy of Holies defiled. There were a series of prescribed ceremonial and physical cleansing necessary before putting on the special garments for entering the Holy Place. It is unmistakable that this priest had done everything possible to be clean, but all his righteousness looked like filthy rags in contrast to the beautiful holiness of God Almighty.

The accuser of the brethren, as Satan is called in the New Testament, immediately challenged this priest's right to minister before God. Joshua was without an answer, but the LORD rebuked Satan. It was sort of, "Oh, shut up!"

Even though Satan was silenced, his accusation was correct. The LORD handled it by having the priest stripped of his filthy clothes [self-righteousness?] and called for one of His own robes to be brought and put on the priest. Joshua then stood before Jehovah clothed in the righteousness of Christ Jesus.

This is how the Lord handles our unrighteousness. He strips us of all that is defiled, and covers us with His own garments that are ultimate righteousness. Another prophet, Isaiah, saw this same provision, for he wrote:

> *No weapon that is formed against thee shall prosper; and every tongue that shall rise against thee in judgment thou shalt condemn. This is the heritage of the servants of the LORD,* ***and their righteousness is of me, saith the LORD.***[20]

Similarly, when John saw the Bride of Christ in heaven he said, "*Fine linen, bright and clean, was given her to wear. (Fine linen stands for the righteous acts of the saints*)."[21]

The Procurement of Righteousness

We need righteousness if we are to minister as believer priests. But any righteousness we could produce is unacceptable to God as being too far beneath His standards. He calls our righteousness "*filthy rags*" (Isaiah 4:6). However, God has provided an ample supply of divine righteousness through our Lord Jesus Christ. The big question, then, is how do we get it and how do we maintain it? Paul taught us: "*For in the gospel a righteousness from God is revealed, a righteousness that is by faith from first to last, just as it is written: 'The righteous will live by faith.'*"[22]

Paul learned this through experience. A religious zealot, he sought for years to produce a righteous life by rigid observance of the law. He persecuted the church in his zeal, even becoming the cause of the death of many Christians. When he met Jesus on the road to Damascus, he was re-instructed, regenerated, and clothed with imputed righteousness. All Paul had to do was believe what Jesus said to him. The righteousness came to him when faith reached out to Christ Jesus.

The steps of Paul's transformation from a religious bigot persecutor to a righteous believer priest can be told in three phrases:

1. **Imparted faith**. When Jesus spoke to him, faith was imparted, for "*Faith cometh by hearing, and hearing by the word of God.*"[23] We cannot produce faith for righteousness. We must receive it as a gift from God. We do not invent the faith for righteousness; God imparts it to us through His word. God believes everything He says, and if we listen closely we will find that faith is being imparted to us as we hear Him speak.

2. **Personal acceptance**. We believer priests need to know that if God said it, that settles it. We don't have to feel it; we don't have to produce it; we merely have to accept it as a fact. As with Paul, believing what God tells us in His Word often requires us to walk away from some religious training in our past. All our training in righteousness by works will have to be discounted before we will be able to personally accept righteousness as a garment given by Christ Jesus.

3. **Change of mind**. Jesus appeared to Paul, spoke to him, blinded him for a season, sent a prophet to restore that sight, and gave him a commission from the Lord, but only Paul could actually change his mind. This is where many of us believers fail. We respond to the emotion Christ's intervention produces, but we don't expend the necessary energy to adjust our thinking. Consequently, when the emotion is exhausted, we are still in the old mind-set. Little wonder, then, that God challenges us: "*Do not conform any longer to the pattern of this world, but be transformed* ***by the renewing of your mind****. Then you will be able to test and approve what God's will is—his good, pleasing and perfect will.*"[24]

Somewhere in the lives of believer priests, there must come a mind change that believes what God has said about them, not what their conscience says or what the enemy may say.

The priest in times of worship is supposed to deal with God, not with himself. He has cleansed himself from sin and defilement before he even put on his priestly garment. Now he must accept his standing in God as a consecrated priest clothed in the righteousness of Christ with a right and a responsibility to approach the throne of grace to worship God.

Yet, there is probably no other time in the life of a believer priest when he faces such inner condemnation as when he begins to approach God in worship. The awesome holiness of God is like a giant magnifying mirror that reflects every flaw in our nature. We become introspective and begin to deal with ourselves, our failures, our short comings, and our inabilities.

As in Zechariah's vision of Joshua standing before God being accused by Satan, our right of entrance to God's throne will consistently be challenged. That intended impeachment is consistently based on our unrighteous behavior—"*filthy garments.*" We are repeatedly told that we are not worthy. So what's new? Remember what a large percentage of persons approaching Jesus used as an introductory remark—"I am not worthy." This is so consistent with persons who have not yet learned to appropriate God's righteousness by faith that Paul wrote: "*With this in mind, we constantly pray for you, that our **God may count you worthy** of his calling, and that by his power he may fulfill every good purpose of yours and every act prompted by your faith.*"[25]

The word "count" is an accountant's term. It is an entrance into the ledger. God puts His righteousness to the credit column of our ledger. He declares us righteous. He makes a deposit of righteousness in our account. Rather than lament at our lack of right standing before God, we should merely write a check on God's deposit to our account. Faith in God's provision enables us to get our eyes off ourselves and onto Himself. There will be no worship until this occurs.

Believer priests need to remember that imparted faith, followed by personal acceptance and a change of mind will bring them into God's imputed righteousness. We don't work our way in—we believe our way in. The Bible puts it: "*This righteousness from God comes through faith in Jesus Christ to all who believe. There is no difference.*"[26]

Your culture doesn't matter. It is to "*all who believe.*" Religious background doesn't matter. "*Righteousness from God comes through faith . . . to all who believe*"—Christian works or lack of them doesn't matter. It is "*to all who believe.*" It is faith in God's provision and promise that brings Christ's robe of righteousness as a replacement for your defilement.

We are all familiar with the beloved Shepherd Psalm—Psalm 23. It promises that "*He guides me in paths of righteousness for his name's sake.*"[27] God not only offers His righteousness for a mere response of faith, He also guides us in the ways of righteousness so that we think righteous thoughts, do righteous deeds, and live righteous lives. He does not merely give us an instruction book, although the Bible is that. By His Spirit, He lives in us to demonstrate and direct that righteousness in His believer priests.

The fundamental responsibility of the believer priest is to worship the Lord, but Who is this Lord that we worship? Twice the prophet Jeremiah answers this question by stating: "*This is the name by which he will be called:* ***The LORD Our Righteousness****.*"[28] That is one of the covenant names of God. Not God the righteous, but God "*our righteousness.*" How glorious it is that the object of our worship is also the source of our righteousness in which we worship.

We have prepared to function as priests in establishing our eligibility. We have the equipment for worship, for we've built our altar. We've found entrance to God's presence through His provided righteousness. Now it is time to get involved with the elements of worship. It is time to praise the Lord!

Believer priests, get your eyes off yourselves and onto the One we serve in worship. Join David in declaring, "*My tongue will speak of your righteousness and of your praises all day long.*"[29]

Chapter 5 Endnotes

1. Isaiah 64:6, *NIV*, emphasis added

2. 1 Corinthians 6:9

3. Psalm 132:9, *NIV*

4. Isaiah 61:10, *NIV*

5. Matthew 22:12-14

6. Romans 6:19, *NIV*, emphasis added

7. Lawrence O. Richards, *Expository Dictionary of Bible Words*, 1985 Zondervan Press, p. 533, Grand Rapids, MI.

8. 1 Samuel 15:22, *NIV*

9. Deuteronomy 6:25, *NIV*, emphasis added

10. Romans 5:17, *NIV*, emphasis added

11. 1 Corinthians 1:30

12. Romans 8:3-4, *NIV*

13. Matthew 5:17, *NIV*

14. Romans 1:11, *NIV*

15. 1 Corinthians 11:23-24

16. Romans 4:20-24

17. Oswald Chambers, *The Best From All His Books*, Volume II, page 267. Oliver-Nelson Books, 1989, Nashville, TN

18. Oswald Chambers, *The Best From All His Books*, Volume II, page 293. Thomas Nelson, Inc., Publishers, 1987, Nashville, TN

19. Zechariah 3:1-5, *NIV*

20. Isaiah 54:17, emphasis added

21. Revelation 19:8, *NIV*

22. Romans 1:17, *NIV*

23. Romans 10:17

24. Romans 12:2, *NIV*, emphasis added

25. 2 Thessalonians 1:11, *NIV*, emphasis added

26. Romans 3:22, *NIV*

27. Psalm 23:3, *NIV*

28. Jeremiah 23:6; 33:16, *NIV*

29. Psalm 35:28, *NIV*

6
The Entrance of the Priesthood
The Believer Priest's Praise

It should be self-evident that no priest can serve until he is at the place of service. For believer priests, that place is the presence of the Lord. The oft quoted Psalm 100 says that we should, "*Enter into his gates with thanksgiving, and into his courts with praise: be thankful unto him, and bless his name*" (verse 4). Believer priests shouldn't approach God with problems and petitions. We come before Him with praise.

The great hymn of the Bible exults, "*Serve the LORD with gladness: come before his presence with singing.*"[1] It is difficult to think of a priest, even a believer priest, without visualizing service. After all, the priest is a servant of God. He performs an *ecclesia* ministry —service to the people on God's behalf. All the service of a believer priest should be a joyful, melodious service. What we often overlook is that the priest's first service must be unto God. He is first and foremost a worshiper. His praise to and of God is more important than his performance of ritualistic service for the people.

When the devil tempted Jesus in the matter of worship, Jesus answered him, "*Thou shalt worship the Lord thy God, and him only shalt thou serve.*"[2] This not only proved to be the quotation of Scripture that ended the temptation, it became the pattern of response to God for all believer priests. Worship first; service second. Until we have fulfilled the worship requirement, we cannot serve properly. "All service must flow out of worship lest it become a substitute for worship. We long ago learned that God will curse a substitute, but may bless a supplement. . .It is not an 'either/or' situation but a 'both/and'. We will both worship and serve the Lord God; but in that order."[3]

If the purpose of a priesthood is to restore relationship between people and God, we must remind ourselves that God's desire for this restored relationship is for personal pleasure. God really doesn't need our service. What can we do for God that He could not do with one word from His mouth? What God really desires from us is not a host of slaves working in His fields, but the *Hallelujahs* of redeemed persons singing His praise.

The psalmist affirms, "*For the LORD taketh pleasure in his people*" (Psalm 149:4). God finds delight not in our performance, but in our personhood. It is not our labors on His behalf that pleases Him. It is our love expressed unto Him that gives Him such great pleasure. Several years ago I wrote an article for *New Wine Magazine* in which I stated, "Somewhere along the line, the church has forgotten that this is what gives pleasure to God. We are the object of His joy and our praise is the satisfaction of His own heart."[4]

Praise is not a sub-topic of the Bible; it is actually a main topic. There is no Bible doctrine mentioned more often than the command to praise. "*Praise, praised, praising*" are mentioned over 280 times in the *King James Version of the Bible. The New International Version* lists the word "praise" 340 times.

In conferences on praise, it has been interesting to watch the reaction of people when I have presented the following contrasts between the number of times seven basic Bible doctrines are mentioned in the Bible versus seven methods of expressing praise. We have built denominations to promulgate some of these doctrines. We raise millions of dollars annually to implement others. We have made a sacrament of baptism, and preach fervently on the second coming of Christ Jesus, and this is good and proper. But none of these truths are emphasized in the Bible as frequently as praise unto God. Look at the contrasts:

Fundamental Doctrines	Times Mentioned	Methods of Praise	Times Mentioned
The Virgin Birth	2	Dancing	5
Missions	12	Shouting	65
Justification	70	Thanksgiving	135
Sanctification	72	Singing	287
Baptism	80	Rejoicing	288
Repentance	110	Playing instruments	317
Second Coming of Christ	318	Praise	340 (NIV)

Perhaps the great preponderance of emphasis on praise is because that is something we must do, while the fundamental doctrines are teachings of what God has done for us. Somehow it is consistently more difficult for God to get us to do for Him than to receive what He has done for us.

It should be self-evident that we believer priests must be grounded in sound doctrine. How can we be teaching priests if we don't know what we believe and why we believe it? Doctrine should be the guidelines of our lives and ministries. As valuable and valid as doctrine is, in the Bible the expression of our love for God is treated far more widely than the teachings of doctrine. Believer priests must be more than students of God's Word. We must be stupendous praisers as well. We cannot live exclusively in our intellect. Our hearts must be allowed opportunities to flow articulations of adoration and praise unto God to Whom the doctrines point. Priestly service that is based entirely on principle tends to become calloused and cold. We need the warmth of praise in our lives and ministries. Let's add a shout to our sacrifices, a praise to our priestly performance, and a rejoicing in our ritual. Could we dare dance in the midst of our duties?

I sat in a restaurant in New Mexico one evening recently. The waitress who was serving customers across the dining room seemed exuberantly joyful. She did not walk from table to table, she danced. It was child-like and quite unprofessional, but it induced a joyful attitude among the diners. I prayed as I watched her, "Lord, help me to be equally uninhibited when serving You in public."

In my vast teaching on praise, I have met considerable resistance based on how little the New Testament seems to teach about praising God. The New Testament does not teach a great deal on praise because it does not need to. Praise was a distinctive, heavenly set ministry in the Old Testament. As we came into a New Testament age, the worship of God did not cease; it was greatly amplified with the presence of Jesus and became so much more personal and real. The Holy Spirit in the lives of individual believers gave meaning to and motivation for the forms and rituals of worship the Old Testament had taught. These New Testament believers did not need a new pattern for praise; they merely needed fresh purpose and power in their praise.

TOWDAH — Thanksgiving Praise

It has been observed that while English is a great language for culture, science, and business communication, it is a weak language for expressing feelings. For instance, we have but one word for "love," and it may mean lust, like, appreciation, fondness, or deep affection. We are very dependent upon the context of the sentence to know what the word "love" means.

Similarly, we have but one word for "praise," but there are seven Hebrew words for praise in the Old Testament that form a pattern of movement towards God. Some see them as a liturgical order for the priests ascending the hill of Zion where the Ark of the Covenant was kept in a tent. Perhaps these same seven words can form the steps we believer priests can take when coming into the realized presence of God.

The first of these words is *towdah*—"a sacrifice of thanksgiving that is demonstrated with an extension of the hands in adoration and acceptance."[5] There is the implication of the hands being extended with the palms cupped in an upward position. It is used for thanking God for things not yet received as well as for things already at hand. It is the sacrifice of thanksgiving. *Towdah* praise is the sacrifice of thanksgiving. That is the bottom line of *towdah* praise. There actually are only two times believer priests should praise the Lord—when we feel like it and when we don't feel like it. There are times when the emotion of thanksgiving and rejoicing almost automatically spill over into praise, and there are other times when we sense no positive feelings towards God. That's when we need to get our hands in the air and offer the sacrifice of thanksgiving—*towdah*. It is activating ourselves to rejoice in what is guaranteed by God's Word though it may not have taken place yet.

There is an element of faith in the sacrifice of thanksgiving. It anticipates. It is *towdah*; it knows that if it will take its place in the presence of God, it will be rewarded for that very thing.

God promised Jeremiah that "*I will hasten my word to perform it.*"[6] God is still watching over His Word to perform it. When a believer steps into the presence of God by faith and begins to lift his heart unto the Lord with a sacrifice of thanksgiving—not necessarily wanting to do it—not feeling emotionally released to do it—often almost too weary to do it—God sees his heart struggling clumsily to obey Him and He watches over His Word to perform it in that individual's behalf. God responds to a sacrifice of praise.

Brother Asaph, the psalmist, used this word when he wrote, "*Whoso offereth praise glorifies me: and to him that ordereth his conversation aright will I shew the salvation of God.*"[7]

Paraphrased, Asaph said, "Whoever offers praise—the person who lifts his or her hands to me palms cupped inward, *towdah*—who sacrifices thanksgiving whether or not he or she feels like it, sacrifices to Me—glorifies Me." To this person God guarantees salvation or wholeness. This is reinforced in the *New International Version of the Bible*. It reads, "*He who sacrifices thank offerings honors me, and he prepares the way so that I may show him the salvation of God.*"[8] Eugene Peterson's translation reads: "*It's the praising life that honors me. As soon as you set your foot on the Way, I'll show you my salvation.*"[9]

This word *towdah* is widely used in the Old Testament. It is the title for Psalm 100 that has become a pattern of worship for thousands of believers. It is the word the prophet used when he described what he saw in the Spirit after the captivity of Babylon. He wrote: "*And they shall come . . . bringing burnt offerings, and sacrifices, and meat offerings, and incense, and bringing sacrifices of praise, unto the house of the LORD.*"[10] The first five verses of Psalm 42 are all *towdah* verses, as is Psalm 56:12 and 75:9. David sang out: "*Sing unto God, sing praises (towdah) to his name: Extol him that rideth upon the heavens by his name JAH, and rejoice before him.*"[11] Obviously God wants us to get into the sacrifice of praise and, if need be, even rejoice and dance before Him whether we feel like it or not. That's the desire of the heart of God, for God wants us to learn that praise is not extended on the basis of our emotions or feelings. It is extended on the simple basis of a mind set that says He is worthy of our praise.

If we are to "*ascend into the hill of the Lord*"[12]—come into God's realized presence—we must take the initiative. It is one thing for us to pray for God to come to us, but God's provision is for us to come to Him. The first step towards God's presence is when the priest, by a deliberate act of his or her will, lifts holy hands heavenward and begins to offer a sacrifice of praise to Almighty God.

Towdah praise teaches us that the lifting up of hands—palms cupped inward, with the opening of our lips in verbal expression of praise regardless of our present emotion, and, perhaps, the quoting of Scripture—is a very acceptable sacrifice of praise. It is a logical beginning of a worship pattern for all believer priests.

Whatever significance we may place on the raising of hands, we priests dare not forget its two elementary purposes. It is a sign of need and it is a sign of surrender. It demonstrates the initial attitude of a priest of God. The upraised, cupped hands say, "Holy Spirit, I have a need. I am empty. Please fill my cup." Those hands raised also say, "I surrender—You win." David likens the lifting of the hands to the evening sacrifice when he writes, "*May my prayer be set before you like incense; may the lifting up of my hands be like the evening sacrifice.*"[13] It really doesn't take much energy to cup your hands and lift them to God to say in body language, "I praise You, I surrender to You, I need You." God responds to this early form of praise!

YADAH — Power Praise

As precious as this is, it is but the first step in coming into the presence of God to worship. The second step is illustrated with the Hebrew word *yadah*. It, too, refers to the position of our hands, but not now in the form of a cup asking for something. "It is the action of extending of our hands in power as we confess, praise, sing, and give thanks to the nature and work of God."[14] *Yadah* pictures the extension of our hands with all our strength. We might call it the power salute.

Frequently as we priests obediently lift our cupped hands in a sacrifice of praise to God, there comes a refreshing. We feel stronger in the spirit and with the hands turn outward, we move from supplication to salutation. We begin to stretch our arms into the presence of God and to rejoice with *yadah* praise. The tiredness and reluctance disappear in the freshness of God's presence. There comes a flush or a pulsation of strength through our beings in this ascending ministry we have when coming before the throne of heaven.

Whereas *towdah* praise can flow completely as an act of dedication that becomes a sacrifice of praise, *yadah* praise is a beginning response to the presence of the Lord. He has responded to our sacrifice of praise, and now we are reacting to His response. We have begun to move from the mind to the heart. The psalmist understood this, for he wrote: "*I will praise the LORD with my whole heart, in the assembly of the upright, and in the congregation.*"[15] The Hebrew word for "praise" in this verse is *yadah*. The raising of his hands now came from an emotion in his heart. It was done enthusiastically, forcefully, and publicly.

This word *yadah* is frequently used in the Old Testament and is consistently translated "praise." It is often coupled with explanatory words such as "greatly," "with song," "with my whole heart," etc.[16]

HALAL — Celebration Praise

This inner sense of strength that causes us to throw our hands upward toward God logically leads to the third expression of praise—*halal*. The word is "a primary root meaning to be clear; to shine; hence to make a show; to boast; to be bright, to be splendid; to praise; to celebrate, to glorify."[17] *Strong's Hebrew Dictionary* adds, "It is to be clamorously foolish." It's the most common expression of praise found in the Scriptures. It is the root of the word *hallelujah—halal to Jah*—hallelujah. To *halal* is to hallelujah in the presence of the Lord. It is praise to Jehovah. It is to celebrate, to shine, to boast, or to rave about Yah, God. The psalmists loved to use this word. One wrote, "*Let my soul live, and it shall praise [halal] thee; and let thy judgments help me.*"[18] Perhaps we could translate this verse simply, "Let my soul live and it will go bananas in Your presence."

The psalter ends with ten injunctions to praise the Lord and every time the word "praise" occurs, it is the Hebrew word *halal*. *Halal* God in His sanctuary. *Halal* God in the firmament of His power. *Halal* God for His mighty acts. *Halal* with the trumpet. *Halal* with the harp. *Halal* God in the dance (Psalm 150). Every time the word *halal* is used, it suggests that we celebrate, boast, and be clamorously foolish before God. Today this kind of behavior is found in the sports arenas and celebrity concerts, but it belongs in church.

Halal is not a private form of praise. We are to "[halal]—*Thee among the people.*"[19] We're even enjoined to "*Praise Him* [halal] *in the assembly of the elders.*"[20] Maybe if we believer priests could get enthusiastic about the God we serve, our enthusiasm might draw others to approach the hill of the Lord with us.

David declared: "*My mouth shall praise* [halal] *thee with joyful lips.*"[21] We believer priests need to learn to do the same thing. Let our mouths pour forth joyful praise in a most exuberant way, even if we appear to be clamorously foolish before God.

ZAMAR — Melodious Praise

This Hebrew word means "to touch the strings or parts of a musical instrument, i.e., to play upon it; to make music, accompanied by the voice; hence to celebrate in song and music." It also means "to harp on chords, to play, to make music, to sing, to sing praises, to celebrate."[22] It obviously has to do with musical praise, both vocal and instrumental.

David not only sang unto the Lord, he played music on his harp. He invented musical instruments, and imported special wood for the construction of instruments. He trained and set, in the service of God, an orchestra of musicians to play before the Ark of the Lord every hour of the day. This great worshiper of God knew the important place music plays in releasing praise from our inner spirits.

His students learned well, for we read, "*Sing to the Lord with thanksgiving: make music to our God on the harp.*"[23] It means to sing with instrumental accompaniment. Another student wrote: "*I will sing a new song unto thee, O God: upon a psaltery and an instrument of ten strings will I sing praises unto thee.*"[24]

All believer priests eventually learn that there is a level of praise attained when it is released melodiously that may not be achieved without music. Music unites our thinking, feeling, vocabulary, and our focus. It enables us to respond to God as a unit rather than as disconnected individuals. What a service musical believer priests can perform for other less talented priests. Pave a way into the presence of God with your instrumental worship of God. Zamar God!

BARAK— Adoration Praise

As believer priests continue their ascent in praise, they come across the Hebrew word *barak*. It basically means, "to kneel; to bless God (as an act of adoration); kneel down; praise."[26] It is the Hebrew word for hope, but it is translated "praise" three times.

Barak praise is in contrast to the exuberant *zamar* praise in that it is usually an act of adoration. Often in *barak* nothing at all is spoken. It's the "*Be still, and know that I am God*"[27] form of praise. It is waiting quietly in God's presence while our attitude of heart is checked. In *barak* worship, we choose to wait quietly in His presence for Him to work. There is a waiting season in the praise approach to God, but that waiting should always be in hope—*barak*.

There is a time to shout our praises from the housetops, and there is equally a time to quietly bow in adoration before His presence. Usually we have to shout our emotions into submission before we can wait adoringly in His presence, but we shouldn't shout and run. We must learn to bellow and bow—to shout and kneel. Just as noise in worship is threatening to some believer priests, silence is threatening to others. We are not invited to choose our style. We all need the times of emotional response in praise, and we also need times of quite reverence and quietness in our worship.

TEHILLAH — Singing Praise

The Hebrew-Greek Key Study Bible defines *tehillah* as "A song of praise (a technical musical term for a song which exults God); a psalm (the title to the entire book of Psalms is in the plural form). Laudation in song, to sing in the spirit or from the spirit, an ode of the spirit, a psalm in both its written and pre-written state. *Tehillah* occurs fifty-seven times."[28]

This sixth word for praise is more than a type of song; it is the residual song of your spirit. It refers to the free-form of praise singing that many today call "the song of the Lord." These extemporaneous songs are *tehillah* and out of this *tehillah* singing many of the psalmists wrote the songs down when they heard them being sung and they became the *tehillam* (the Hebrew title for the book of Psalms).

Tehillah means to sing in the Spirit, whether in tongues or from the residue of our own spirit. Paul said: "*I will sing with the spirit, and I will sing with the understanding also.*"[29] David wrote, "*He hath put a new song in my mouth even praise* [tehillah]."[30] David was comfortable with this form of singing—a heart that improvises its own lyrics and melody in expressing praise to God.

In my first book I wrote:

> As valuable as it is for us to use the songs of others, while learning a praise vocabulary, the Spirit within us would like to release the singing of a "new song"—that which is particularly expressive of you and your experience. Don't hesitate in releasing new songs during your praise time. God delights in hearing the "new song." . . .
>
> Singing the Scriptures can become double-praising. There is the melodious release of the inner feelings plus the anointed words of the Bible. What melody? Well, there are many traditional tunes, but if you don't happen to know any, just lean on the Holy Spirit. Start and see what happens. You may be very happily surprised! When I began singing Psalm 150, I started to feel what the author felt and to sense and see what he was experiencing, and soon I was responding as the writer was responding to God's goodness. In times of pressure, instead of turning on your television or going to the refrigerator, take the Word, read aloud one of the Psalms, and declare it to be the expression of your own heart to God. . . .

> Singing "with the Spirit" refers not only to singing a song inspired by the Spirit, but singing in the language of the Spirit. This language of the Spirit has not come as a prayer language only, but also as a praise language. Don't be afraid to release that language melodiously. How I used to thrill hearing our congregation sing in the Spirit, using a variety of languages and rising and falling in pitch as though all knew the song ahead of time. The conscious mind seemed to be bypassed, and the spirit within was unhampered in releasing praise unto the Lord.
>
> It is not unusual for a person given to praise to awaken in the middle of the night aware that the Spirit within him is praising the Lord in song. If our conscious mind did not establish such a rigorous censorship, I would not be surprised if this would occur frequently during the waking hours too.[31]

We quite commonly quote, "*But thou art holy, O thou that inhabitest the praises of Israel*."[32] The word translated "praises" is *tehillah. The New International Version of the Bible* substitutes, quite accurately, the word "enthroned" for "inhabitest." God is enthroned upon the residual song of the spirits of His people. Oh how we believer priests need to lift our hands and sing freely from our spirits in the congregation. That is what God inhabits. That is where God is enthroned. If we will build His throne, He will be seated in our midst.

This word *tehillah* is found in several passages in the Bible. Isaiah used it when he spoke prophetically for God: "*Behold, I will do a new thing; now it shall spring forth; shall ye not know it? I will even make a way in the wilderness, and rivers in the desert. . . . This people have I formed for myself; they shall show forth my praise* [tehillah]."[33] When God does a new thing among His people, it inspires new songs. As beautiful as the songs of past generations may be, the most expressive songs are the songs the Spirit sings in the midst of a fresh visitation of God among His people. God's believer priests need to be open to contemporary songs that express joy and praise in the language of today's generation.

Tehillah praise is not optional. It is commanded! We read, "*Sing forth the honour of his name: make his praise* [tehillah] *glorious.*"[34] It is not a matter of waiting until the Holy Spirit initiates a song within us. We, the believer priests, make His praise glorious. We can activate that song in our own spirits and sing a song of our hearts. This Psalm indicates that we're to work at it until we can make it glorious in the presence of the Lord. We need not be qualified and talented musicians to make this praise glorious. It is the uniqueness and individuality of the song that give it glory. It is the fervor of the priest's heart that excites the heart of God.

It doesn't seem that God expects *tehillah* praise to be a rare exception. David sang, "*I will bless the Lord at all times. His praise,* [tehillah] *shall continually be in my mouth.*"[35] Believer priests, there should be a constant singing in our spirits. From time to time throughout the day, we should vocalize what has been internalized all day long. The Holy Spirit makes our spirits singing spirits.

The New Testament espouses this same teaching. We are commanded: "*Be not drunk with wine, wherein is excess; but be filled with the Spirit; Speaking to yourselves in psalms and spiritual songs, singing and making melody in your heart to the Lord.*"[36] Being filled with the Spirit is a progressive act. The literal Greek says, "*keep being filled with the Spirit.*" This means our song should never expire. It should be renewed daily as we are daily renewed in the Holy Spirit.

There are three classifications of song given in this injunction. Paul speaks first of **Psalms**—songs of praise from Scripture, songs in the character, spirit, or manner of Old Testament psalms. These songs are directed primarily to God. Second, Paul lists the singing of **hymns** that are songs of praise of human composition on Christian themes. These are directed primarily to man as testimonies or boasting of God. The third class of singing in this passage are called **spiritual songs**.

These are songs of praise of a spontaneous or unpremeditated nature with unrehearsed melodies, sung under the impetus of the Holy Spirit. They may be directed to both God and man. This type of singing is the equivalent of the Old Testament word *tehillah*.

Sam Sasser, co-author of this book, tells of accidentally finding an old copy of *The Epistles of Polycarp* in the Fuller Theological Library while doing research for his doctorate degree. You may remember that Polycarp was a young aristocrat who John led to the Lord shortly before his death at 98 years of age. Polycarp became one of the early church fathers and was a leader of the early church. He declared that the early Christian martyrs sang *tehillah* praise in the arenas as they awaited death. He wrote, "This day we rejoice for even as many of our brothers and sisters are led into the arenas and fed to the lions and our hearts cringe and we cry out for them, yet as they stand waiting to be gnawed by the beasts, they lift their hands and they sing the residual song of their spirit, the *tehillah*, and there are more in the stands of the arena repenting and coming to Christ than the numbers we are losing to the lions."[37] What a testimony to the power of this song of the Spirit.

But you say, I couldn't fake such a song. You don't need to. The Bible says "*He is thy praise*,"[38] and the word used is *tehillah*. This residual song of the spirit is not something that is conjured up; God is the substance of it. When we lift our voice to sing extemporaneously unto God, He becomes the subject, the motivation, and the inspiration of our song. At times, He actually joins us in such singing, for the prophet declared, "*The LORD thy God in the midst of thee is mighty; he will save, he will rejoice over thee with joy; he will rest in his love, he will joy over thee with singing*."[39] God delights in singing joyful melodies with and in us, and you have never heard such singing as He can do. [For other verses using the word *tehillah*, see footnote [40]]

SHABACH — Shouting Praise

The study Bible we have been quoting for definitions of these seven Hebrew words for praise says that *shabach* is "a primary root; to address in a loud tone, i.e., triumph—to be loud. There are eleven occurrences of this word in the Hebrew Old Testament."[41]

Sometimes when God joins the congregation in their *tehillah* praise, the joyful emotion of the congregation erupts into a shout of victory, and that shout can become thunderous. This form of praise is *shabach* praise. When jubilation of faith wells up in a believer priest's spirit, a shout is the only honest expression that will release it. Some things just cannot be whispered. They must be shouted.

We can't always be defending our faith. There comes a time when we need to celebrate it. God delights in celebration. The Old Testament is full of it. David exclaimed, "*Because thy lovingkindness is better than life, my lips shall praise* [shabach] *thee*."[42] He also wrote, "*Shout unto God with a voice of triumph*,"[43] and "*Let them shout for joy and be glad. Let the Lord be magnified*."[44] [Other uses of the word *shabach* can be found in footnote[45]].

Believer priests, there are seven steps that will bring us into the presence of the Lord— that enable us to climb the hill to the ark of the covenant. They are progressive and greatly expressive. We've looked at *towdah*, the sacrifice of thanksgiving. As the mind becomes collected and we begin to press further, we *yadah*, or put the hands up in the power salute. Third, we rise to *halal*, the wave, the celebration, the rejoicing, the being clamorously foolish in the presence of the Lord. Often the dance begins at this juncture. It is a logical step then to *zamar* where the instruments accompany our singing and the instrumentalist enjoy praise with us. Sometimes it is a surprise to us, but the next step is often *barak* where we get quiet before God and kneel in His presence. We then can rise to *tehillah* as we release the residual song of our spirit that may cause us to shout the *shabach* shout of victory in the presence of God.

Walking in these steps of praise will enlarge us and mature us as believer priests.

Chapter 6 Endnotes

1.Psalm 100:2

2.Matthew 4:10

3.Judson Cornwall, "Worship," *New Wine Magazine*, November 1976, page 7

4.Judson Cornwall, *New Wine Magazine*, December 1972, page 57

5.Zohiates, Spiros, *The Hebrew-Greek Key Study Bible*, AMG Publishers, Chattanooga, TN 1986

6.Jeremiah 1:12

7.Psalm 50:23

8.Psalm 50:23, *NIV*

9.Psalm 50:23, *The Message: Psalms*, Eugene H. Peterson. NavPress, Colorado Springs, CO 80915

10.Jeremiah 17:26

11.Psalm 68:4

12.Psalm 24:3

13.Psalm 141:2, *NIV.* 1973, 1978, 1984 by International Bible Society

14.Zohiates, Spiros, *The Hebrew-Greek Key Study Bible*. AMG Publishers Chattanooga, TN

15.Psalm 111:1

16.Psalm 28:6-8; 30:12; 33:2; 42:5; 43:5; 86:12; 107:8; 109:30; 111:1; 107:8, and others.

17.Zohiates, Spiros, *The Hebrew-Greek Key Study Bible*. AMG Publishers, Chattanooga, TN

18.Psalm 119:175

19.Psalm 63:5

20.Psalm 35:18

21.Psalm 107:32

22.Zohiates, Spiros, *The Hebrew-Greek Key Study Bible*. AMG Publishers, Chattanooga, TN

23.Psalm 147:7, *NIV.* 1973, 1978, 1984 by International Bible Society

24.Psalm 144:9

25.Judson Cornwall, *Let Us Praise*, pages 84-85. 1973 by Logos International, Plainfield, NJ

26.Zohiates, Spiros, *The Hebrew-Greek Key Study Bible*. AMG Publishers, Chattanooga, TN

27.Psalm 46:10

28.Zohiates, Spiros, *The Hebrew-Greek Key Study Bible*. AMG Publishers, Chattanooga, TN

29.1 Corinthians 14:15

30.Psalm 40:3

31.Judson Cornwall, *Let Us Praise*, pages 85-86. 1973 by Logos International, Plainfield, NJ

32.Psalm 22:3

33.Isaiah 43:19, 21

34Psalm 66:2

35.Psalm 34:1

36.Ephesians 5:18-19

37.The Epistles of Polycarp

38.Deuteronomy 10:21

39.Zephaniah 3:17

40.Psalms 9:14; 22:25; 33:1; 34:1; 66:8; 71:6; 71:8; 71:14; 100:4

41.Zohiates, Spiros, *The Hebrew-Greek Key Study Bible*. AMG Publishers, Chattanooga, TN

42.Psalm 63:3

43.Psalm 47:1

44.Psalm 35:27

45.Psalms 63:3; 145:4; 147:12

7
The Eloquence of the Priesthood
The Believer Priest's Prayers

Assuming we have made all necessary preparations and have walked through the steps of praise that bring us into God's presence, now what? The realized presence of God can be so awesome as to completely overwhelm a believer priest. Just witness the thousands of persons who have, as we put it, "fallen under the power" as a person in touch with God prayed for them. If that limited amount of God's presence can so incapacitate them that they can no longer stand on their feet, what would it be like to really be in God's presence?

I realize that there is a place for silence in the presence of God. The prophet Habakkuk declared, "*But the LORD is in his holy temple: let all the earth keep silence before him.*"[1] That is in the Bible just once, and I believe everyone should do it at least once. In contrast to this, we are encouraged and commanded hundreds of times in the Bible to praise, sing, shout, speak, ask, and talk to God.

In the original pattern, God came into Eden's garden not to overwhelm Adam and Eve, but to communicate with them. I believe that is still God's ultimate desire. He wants fellowship with His believer priests and fellowship requires communication.

What should we do when we find ourselves in God's presence? Talk to Him! We generally refer to this as prayer. The prophet Jeremiah assures us that if we initiate communication with God, He will respond by talking with us. He wrote, "*Call to me and I will answer you and tell you great and unsearchable things you do not know.*"[2] How much spiritual ignorance would be dispelled if we would talk to God and allow Him to talk to us.

The Bible calls this talking with God "prayer," but most Christians equate prayer with asking favors of God. Perhaps it would help us to look at ten Bible believer priests who prayed a great variety of prayers to God—from simple communication to prayers of extreme covenant. These priests knew how to talk to God.

David's *Prayer of Communication*

Would anyone dispute that David was a believer priest? Although he was never part of the Aaronic priesthood, nor did he come from the tribe of Levi, he was a worshiper of God who knew Jehovah far more intimately than most men in his generation, if not in ours as well.

After David was anointed king, God placed him in the palace to learn leadership under Saul, but Saul's jealousy forced David to flee for his life. While hiding in a wilderness area, he heard that the Philistines consistently raided Keilah and robbed their threshing floors. David asked the Lord whether he should go and deliver the inhabitants of Keilah from the Philistines. God told him "*Go, and smite the Philistines, and save Keilah*"[3] David was victorious and accepted the invitation of the inhabitants of Keilah to move into their walled city.

When Saul heard this, he mustered his army to go capture David. David prayed:

> *O Lord God of Israel . . . will the men of Keilah deliver me up into his hand? will Saul come down, as they servant hath heard? O Lord God of Israel, I beseech thee, tell thy servant. And the Lord said, he will come down. Then said David, Will the men of Keilah deliver me and my men into the hand of Saul? And the Lord said, They will deliver thee up.*[4]

David was communicating with God about natural events. He wasn't talking about heaven or spiritual wonders. He was inquiring about circumstances that would determine his course of action. David needed information that only God could give and God shared with David.

Throughout the Bible, men and women when in the presence of God, have talked with Him about very natural events in life. When a believer priest is in the presence of God, he or she does not need an artificial agenda or a special language. David talked to God as he would talk to one of his scouts. So should we! God is interested in us and will gladly talk with us on any subject that is dear to our hearts at the moment. Relax in God's presence and talk to Him as a friend.

When in prayer, we are not in heaven's courtroom following the procedures of law. We are in the presence of our dearest friend who is interested in every facet of our lives. There is nothing we can say that would shock God. There is no need pressing us that disinterests Him. If it concerns us, it concerns Him. When you are in His presence, talk to Him about it. It is better than worrying about it, and He can answer the questions of our hearts, whether it has to do with the family, the job, our relationships with others, or our understanding of God.

How foolish it is to pay the price to come into His presence and then hide the real feelings of our hearts under the mask of being spiritual. We are natural beings with spiritual qualities. Separating the natural and spiritual attributes may be done theologically, but not practically. One is intertwined with the other. That's why in the Lord's prayer our physical needs are presented along with our spiritual understanding of God and His kingdom.

David wrote spiritual songs, and prayed eloquent prayers, but it all started with simple communication with God about natural things—from sheep, to giants, to King Saul. God is pleased to have His priests learn to be honest when they talk with Him. Honesty is eloquent to God.

Daniel's *Prayer of Confession*

Daniel was a godly man who served Jehovah as a political entity under the reign of three kings and kingdoms in Babylon. In the first year of Darius the Mede, who was made king over the realm of the Chaldeans, Daniel reports: "*I set my face unto the Lord God, to seek by prayer and supplications, with fasting, and sackcloth, and ashes: and I prayed unto the Lord my God, and made my confession . . . .*"[5]

In the verses that follow, Daniel confesses the sins of God's captive people as though they were his own sins. He is very specific in his confession and he seems comfortable that Jehovah will forgive.

One reason so many believer priests are uncomfortable coming into the presence of the Lord is that we probably are never more conscious of sin than when in the presence of the sinless Christ Jesus. His purity acts as a giant magnifying mirror that reflects back to us every blemish, stain, and bruise on our body. While we are aware that He is holy, we are also aware that we are not holy. None of the cosmetics or coats that covered these blemishes and stains from the eyes of others work when in God's presence. The writer of the letter to the Hebrews put it so succinctly:

> *For the word of God is living and active. Sharper than any double-edged sword, it penetrates even to dividing soul and spirit, joints and marrow; it judges the thoughts and attitudes of the heart. Nothing in all creation is hidden from God's sight. Everything is uncovered and laid bare before the eyes of him to whom we must give account.*[6]

We know that Jesus is the living Word of God. It is when we are in His presence that our sin is revealed. This revelation is not to prevent our entrance, for we are already in His presence. Neither is it to condemn, for we have been accepted in His presence. The revelation is to give us an opportunity to admit, confess, and be cleansed of everything that seems sinful when close to God.

Don't hesitate a moment in confessing sin when you become aware of it. Everything necessary to eradicate that sin is present or God would not have revealed it to you. God does not expect you to cleanse yourself when in His presence. He merely wants your permission to clean the sin out of your life. If we'll confess the sin, He will cleanse that sin. That's the promise of 1 John 1:9—"*If we confess our sins, he is faithful and just to forgive us our sins, and to cleanse us from all unrighteousness.*"

The sin we see when in the presence of the Lord is usually sin of attitude, concept, and desire far more than sinful deeds. Jesus said, "*Blessed are the pure in heart: for they shall see God.*"[7] Not one of us is capable of producing a pure heart, but God can and will. His method is to make us aware of the impurity, ask us to confess it, and He then removes it from our lives. Our confession of sin is God's permission to intervene in the situation.

Confession is a positive force; not a negative one. It is God's provision that allows us to start over in an area of our lives. Daniel knew this and he confessed his sins and the sins of his generation in anticipation of the release of the captive Israelites to return to Jerusalem. Confession and repentance releases God to cleanse and restore our lives to His perfect will. This is best done when we have come into the presence of God, for there we can be occupied with the perfect example of righteousness rather than with our unrighteousness. How eloquent this can be!

Jeremiah's *Prayer of Submission*

Jeremiah was the major prophet who remained in the land of Judah after the inhabitants were captured by Nebuchadnezzar. He watched this heathen king carry the inhabitants of Judah to Babylon, and he remained with the small remnant left in the land. He had preached pleadingly for the people to return to the LORD, but they would not. Now they were helpless slaves to Babylon.

In his prayers he cried, "*I know, O LORD, that a man's life is not his own; it is not for man to direct his steps. Correct me, LORD, but only with justice—not in your anger, lest you reduce me to nothing.*"[8] This godly, but persecuted, prophet had learned the futility of man trying to determine his own steps, for we are inherently incapable of self-guidance because we're creatures of today with no knowledge of tomorrow. It is imperative that we leave the guidance in the hands of the One who knows the end from the beginning.

This formed the basis for Jeremiah's prayer of submission. He didn't like his present circumstances. He was greatly distressed by what he saw happening in society around him, but he prayed a prayer of submission to the hand and will of God knowing, as was later written, "*that in all things God works for the good of those who love him, who have been called according to his purpose.*"[9]

Believer priests need to quickly submit their lives and ways to God when in the divine presence. We need to hear ourselves pray as Jesus prayed, "*Nevertheless not my will, but thine, be done.*"[10] We can't have our way and His way. Surrender of our way to God is the first step of walking in God's way. Submission, not struggling, is the secret to a walk of close communion with God.

Prayer that gives orders to God is foolish. We don't have His perspective. We can't see what He sees. We don't understand the plans He has laid for our lives. When we demand our own way, we automatically withdraw from His will and way for us.

Submission to God should not be a struggle, for when we are in His presence, the compulsion is love, not force. Surely we can submit to love, especially to divine love. He has our best interests at heart, and He has the power and authority to bring to pass in us everything He has planned. He said:

> *"For I know the plans I have for you," declares the LORD, "plans to prosper you and not to harm you, plans to give you hope and a future. Then you will call upon me and come and pray to me, and I will listen to you. You will seek me and find me when you seek me with all your heart."*[11]

As immature children, we cannot know the plans God has for our lives. As long as we live as submitted children, those plans will automatically unfold—consistent with our maturing. He is forming our lives; we are simply living them. Because of this, we need to regularly pray prayers of submission, for most of us submit to issues and circumstances far more than we submit to God's overall program for us.

One of the reasons some believer priests spend so much time fighting demonic activity is that they do not live lives fully submitted to God. They are like strays or stragglers to the flock of sheep. Every predator sees them as vulnerable. The apostle said, "*Submit yourselves therefore to God. Resist the devil, and he will flee from you.*"[12] Submission to the will of God is an automatic resisting of the enemy. It is also the power of authority over the enemy. When will we learn that it is much easier to submit to God than to struggle with the devil? The old hymn, "*I Surrender All*"[13] needs to be sung or repeated prayerfully every time we come into God's presence. The more completely we surrender to the Lord, the more fully He can work in our lives for His benefit and our blessing. True submission to God has an unspoken eloquence in it.

Elijah's *Prayer of Petition*

Elijah the prophet knew how to pray. In response to his prayer, God shut up the heaven over Israel for three years. This drought so angered King Ahab that Elijah fled the country to save his life.

God made supernatural provision for him in the home of a widow at Zarephath, but after a while, the widow's son died. Elijah "*. . . stretched himself out on the boy three times and cried to the LORD, 'O LORD my God, let this boy's life return to him!' The LORD heard Elijah's cry, and the boy's life returned to him, and he lived.*"[14]

Elijah knew how to petition God for specifics. His relationship with God was so strong that Elijah seemed to know what God's will was and prayed it out loud. From Deuteronomy 11:17, Elijah learned that God had promised to shut the heavens over the land if the people persisted in idolatry. Elijah merely prayed what God had already said. He discovered that there is power in praying God's Word, for that is always the will of God.

Isn't this what the New Testament teaches us? John wrote, "*This is the confidence we have in approaching God: that if we ask anything according to his will, he hears us. And if we know that he hears us—whatever we ask—we know that we have what we asked of him.*"[15]

There is a weakness in making petitionary prayer our primary conversation when we come into the presence of God. We need to linger in the divine presence until we begin to sense what is on God's heart. As we listen to Him speak through His Word or by His Spirit, we come to understand God's will. When we pray in harmony with that will, we have great power in our petition.

God is willing to listen to us express our wills, and He often bends to meet those petitions. However, when we pray what we know to be the will of God, we are praying the most powerful prayers of petition we will ever make.

There is a mystery to prayer that is difficult to define. Why is prayer necessary if God knows everything and already has a predetermined will in the matter? Somehow God has limited Himself in the affairs of mankind to the expressed will of individuals. God will not violate the free moral agency of anyone, but when He is invited, He will intervene in individual lives. Prayer seems to be our way of giving God a right to act. It invests a power of attorney in Him. It says to God, "*your kingdom come, your will be done on earth as it is in heaven.*"[16]

King Ahab had led Israel into deeper and deeper idolatry, yet God's Word had not been fulfilled in producing the judgment of a drought until Elijah came on the scene and pronounced, through prayer, the will of God.

We need to plead God's promises in our prayer times. It is both a provision and a command. Paul wrote: "*Do not be anxious about anything, but in everything, by prayer and petition, with thanksgiving, present your requests to God.*"[17] Anxiety quickly becomes an enemy of faith, and ". . . *without faith it is impossible to please God.*"[18] The best answer to anxiety is faith-filled prayer—"*Cast all your anxiety on him because he cares for you.*"[19] There is no need for us to worry if God has accepted responsibility for our needs.

When in God's presence, talk to Him about what is bothering you. Share your burdens and tell Him about your problems. Just remember that you are not presenting a wish list to a spiritual Santa Claus. You are talking to your Heavenly Father. He responds not out of the immediacy of the need, but out of the intimacy of relationship. A one sentence prayer when in God's presence is worth more than a two page prayer when you are not in His presence. A whisper while resting on His shoulder is better than a shout when involved in the business of daytime activities—and that whisper can be gloriously eloquent.

Moses' *Prayer of Intercession*

Prayers of petition usually involve the needs of the person praying. Moses was capable of this, but he had also learned the power of praying for the needs of others. This praying is called intercession. Moses was a gifted intercessor. He consistently pled with God to change His mind about destroying the rebellious people who had come out of Egypt, but who had not yet let Egypt come out of them. In his first such pleadings with God, Moses told the people:

> *I lay prostrate before the LORD those forty days and forty nights because the LORD had said he would*

> *destroy you. I prayed to the LORD and said, "O Sovereign LORD, do not destroy your people, your own inheritance that you redeemed by your great power and brought out of Egypt with a mighty hand."*[20]

Although we understand that the intercession continued for forty days and nights, the prayer that is recorded is only four verses long. Perhaps this is an extreme condensation or maybe Moses merely repeated it over and over again during this time in God's presence. In these verses, Moses pled God's mercy, His covenants, the coming Calvary, God's glory, and God's responsibility. His intercession was not based on the extreme need of the people, but on the extended mercy of God. He sought to convince God that it was in His best interests to spare the people.

True intercession places the intercessor between God and the problem. It intervenes on behalf of another based on God's faithfulness and His promises. What a glorious ministry this is for a believer priest.

The Old Testament priesthood was in a constant mode of intercession. Every sacrifice the priest offered was a form of intercession. The priest was functioning on behalf of the people, but he was reminding God, through the structured ordinances, that provision had been made to forgive the sins of the people.

When we believer priests are in the presence of God, it is so easy to talk to Him about others. Parents need to consistently remind God of His covenant relationship with their children. Furthermore, we can bring the sick, the oppressed, the depressed, and the sinful to His remembrance with a gentle plea for mercy on their behalf.

Of course, the best intercessor is the Holy Spirit, but He needs a believer priest through whom He can pray. He knows both the mind of God and the true need of the individual for whom we would make intercession. He prays a knowledgeable prayer that is in complete harmony with the will of God. As someone has said, "He talks throne talk." Let Him speak through you when you are in God's presence.

We need to guard against selfishness when in God's presence. Of course we will petition God for our needs and burdens, but we need the inner grace to also talk to Him about others. How are our loved ones going to get saved if we do not become channels of intercession on their behalf? How is revival going to come to our churches if believer priests do not become channels of intercession? It is incongruous for us to expect God to intervene on our behalf if we are unwilling to talk to Him about that intervention. We dare not expect God to answer a prayer that has not been prayed. The promise of Jesus is, "*Ask, and ye shall receive, that your joy may be full.*"[21] The apostle James reminds us, "*Ye have not, because ye ask not.*"[22] The principle of asking as a prerequisite to receiving fits both petitionary prayer and prayers of intercession. When you have praised yourself into God's presence, share with Him your honest concern for others. In that special love relationship, it should be both natural and easy. It will also become eloquent.

Hezekiah's *Prayer of Declaration*

Sometimes our prayers are more declaration of facts than petitions for intervention. Such was the opening of Hezekiah's prayer when the king of Assyria sent him a threatening letter demanding that he surrender Jerusalem to the Assyrian army. We read:

> *Hezekiah received the letter from the messengers and read it. Then he went up to the temple of the LORD and spread it out before the LORD. And Hezekiah prayed to the LORD: "O LORD, God of Israel, enthroned between the cherubim, you alone are God over all the kingdoms of the earth. You have made heaven and earth."*[23]

This godly king then gave God a great deal of "unknown information" about this Assyrian army and their plans to destroy the sacred city.

Did God need this information? Of course not. He knew more about the situation than King Hezekiah knew. It was the king who needed to declare the greatness of God and His authority over all the nations of the earth. This declaration of God's greatness undergirded Hezekiah's faith and calmed his fears. Sometimes we simply need to hear ourselves say what we believe for Jesus said, "*Out of the abundance of the heart the mouth speaketh.*"[24]

The Bible has many such prayers of declaration. David was great in affirming the greatness of God as was Moses and Isaiah. We can't forever be pestering God with our burdens and petty needs. There comes a time when our hearts burst with pride in the greatness of the God Whose presence we are enjoying. We need to join the psalmist in declaring, "*Praise the LORD, O my soul. O LORD my God, you are very great; you are clothed with splendor and majesty.*"[25]

The beauty of prayers of declaration is that it takes our minds off ourselves and focuses our thoughts on the greatness of God. No matter how serious and severe the problem we may be facing, God is far greater than any such problem. Our greatest need is insignificant in His sight. Paul reminds us: "*Now to him who is able to do immeasurably more than all we ask or imagine, according to his power that is at work within us.*"[26] When we declare the greatness of God in our prayers to Him, we enlarge our thinking, release our faith, and delight our God. All of us have a concept of God that is far too small and limited. We need to let those concepts grow up and mature. The longer we serve God, the greater He should become to us. Express that greatness to Him in prayer. As you think it, say it, and hear it you will, as Peter put it, "*Grow in the grace and knowledge of our Lord and Savior Jesus Christ. To him be glory both now and forever! Amen.*"[27]

Two lovers find satisfaction in telling one another how great and wonderful they are. In your love relationship with God, brag on Him. When in His presence, extol His magnificence. Please remember than if you exaggerate beyond your wildest imaginations, you will still be far beneath the true greatness of

God. We cannot overstate the magnificence of God, for we have never seen Him in His fullness. Just always be aware that God is far greater than anything your mouth could ever say of Him. A believer priest will rise to new heights of eloquence when he prays prayers declaring God's greatness.

Asaph's *Prayer of Remembrance*

In Psalm 77, Brother Asaph seems to be in trouble. He is filled with self-pity and given to introspection. In the first six verses, he uses 20 personal pronouns. He has "I" trouble. In his introspection, as is normal, he questions God and draws wrong conclusions about God. He, like many of us, deduced that "*This is my infirmity.*"[28] Fortunately, he appends the conjunction *but* and adds, "*I will remember the years of the right hand of the most High.*"[29]

The moment his prayer turned from self-pity to remembrance of God, he came into victory. He wrote:

> *I will remember the deeds of the LORD; yes, I will remember your miracles of long ago. I will meditate on all your works and consider all your mighty deeds. Your ways, O God, are holy. What god is so great as our God?*[30]

He turned from the inward look to the upward look by simply reminding himself about the wonders of God. So can we!

Occasionally we all fall into the trap of self-examination during times of despair. We find it easy to blame ourselves in seasons of distress. Such introspection will destroy our peace and cause us to question God. In many cases, we are neither the cause of our problem nor the solution to it. The more we examine ourselves, the worse we feel. We need to come up for a fresh breath of air and remind ourselves of better days. It hasn't always been dark. Finances haven't always been so limited. God hasn't always seemed so far away.

Remembrance is a God given tool to extradite ourselves out of the pit of depression. We need to get our minds off our present circumstances and fix them on God. He has been wonderful to us. His mercy has extended to us beyond our fondest dreams. There has been no end to His giving, His loving, and His tender concern for us. As one of the sons of Korah said, "*God is our refuge and strength, an ever-present help in trouble.*"[31] Please remember that it is not that God **was,** but that God **is** a help. All that God ever was, He presently is, for He does not live in the confines of our time-space dimension. He lives in an eternal now. He does not change.

When we remember what God did, we have a pretty good clue to what He is now doing. As William Runyan wrote in his great hymn, "*Thou changeth not, Thy compassions, they fail not; As Thou hast been Thou forever wilt be.*"[32] How great is the faithfulness of our God. Our change of circumstances cannot change His character. He is what He was and will ever be. Remind yourself of your relationship with God in the past and you will find yourself crawling out of the depth of despair. "Remember" must be an important word to God, for it appears 148 times in our Bible. Sometimes we gain a fresh perspective for the future by looking at the past. Time and again we read the phrase, "*Remember what the LORD thy God did . . .*" Try it. It will produce some very positive praying in your life. A positive look backwards can produce some eloquent priestly prayers.

Jonah's *Prayer of Thanksgiving*

Most of us are familiar with Jonah—the disobedient prophet who was swallowed by a giant fish God had prepared. He testified that he spent three days and three nights in the belly of the fish, and Jesus affirmed that this was true.[33] This obviously gave Jonah sufficient time for reflection and repentance. He said, "*When my life was ebbing away, I remembered you, LORD, and my prayer rose to you, to your holy temple.*"[34] Like Asaph, he found that remembering God in prayer helped him rise above his hopeless circumstances.

One would expect Jonah to cry out in pleadings and intercession for God's deliverance, but we read, "*But I, with a song of thanksgiving, will sacrifice to you. What I have vowed I will make good. Salvation comes from the LORD.*"[35] Somewhere in his life Jonah had learned the power of thanksgiving.

From his dark, seaweed infested corner of this fish's belly, Jonah realized that having lived three days and nights in this condition was evidence of God's amazing grace. It is likely that he had done everything possible to get out of this fish, and he realized in his weakened condition that God, and only God, could save him. Summoning all the strength he could muster, Jonah began to offer a sacrifice of thanksgiving unto the Lord. It is difficult to believe that this was a joyful giving of thanks. It was more a desperate, deliberate, decree that responded positively to God's past blessings and present nature. If he died in that fish, he wanted to die thanking God.

There is nothing in the context that even hints that Jonah was trying to get God into a good mood with flowery words. This was not a political ploy. He wasn't "buttering up" God. In spite of his fears, the dangerous and unpleasant circumstances, and the realization that he had brought this judgment upon himself through disobedience, Jonah gave thanks to God. He wanted to leave this world in a chariot of thanksgiving.

We know how the story ended. God was so moved by this display of thanksgiving that He caused the fish to vomit Jonah onto dry land, and the prophet went to Nineveh with God's message for the people.

Anyone can give thanks to God when very positive circumstances surround them, but a true believer priest can thank God in the most adverse circumstances. Paul did. Aboard a ship that was breaking apart in a protracted Euroclydon storm, Paul, having talked with God, "*took bread, and gave thanks to God in presence of them all: and when he had broken it, he began to eat.*"[36] His thanks was not because of, but in spite of, his circumstances. He had received a word from God that invoked a heartfelt thanks to God.

The night before His betrayal, arrest, trial, and subsequent crucifixion, Jesus, "*took bread, and gave thanks, and brake it, and gave unto them, saying, This is my body which is given for you: this do in remembrance of me.*"[37] This had to be a sacrifice of thanksgiving, but it was gloriously accepted by God.

There is no circumstance in life that should prevent our giving thanks to God. Our thanks may be based on a backward look, but it will inspire faith for a forward glance. Complaining seldom changes our circumstances, but thanksgiving almost always changes us in the midst of those unpleasant situations. Paul said, "*In every thing give thanks: for this is the will of God in Christ Jesus concerning you.*"[38] Few prayers sound more eloquent than prayers of thanksgiving when the believer priest is in severe adversity. When in God's presence, give Him thanks!

Hannah's *Prayer of Covenant*

The book of 1 Samuel begins with a touching story of the rivalry between the two wives of Elkanah—Peninnah and Hannah. Hannah was the favorite wife, but she was barren. Peninnah, on the other hand, was very fruitful. Each year this entire family came to the temple to sacrifice unto the Lord in Shiloh. It was supposed to be a festive occasion, but for Hannah it was a miserable time, for Peninnah took delight in goading her about being childless.

On one of these visits Hannah gave herself to earnest, silent prayer—pleading with God for a son. So intent was her praying that Eli, the priest, mistook her for a drunken woman. When he heard the nature of her prayer, he pronounced the blessing of the Lord and a promise that the prayer would be fulfilled.

Hannah's prayer had a quality in it not often heard. She offered to enter into a covenant with God. She prayed, "*O LORD Almighty, if you will only look upon your servant's misery and remember me, and not forget your servant but give her a son, then I will give him to the LORD for all the days of his life, and no razor will ever be used on his head.*"[39] Hannah simply told God that if He would give her what she wanted, she would give it back to Him. She was moving on the principle that if you cannot come to God **with** what He desires, come to God **for** what He desires.

Truthfully, we cannot give to God until He has given to us, for none of us has anything that is useful to God. James reminds us, "*Every good and perfect gift is from above, coming down from the Father of the heavenly lights, who does not change like shifting shadows.*"[40] Good gifts must come down to us before they can be given up to God.

When Jacob was fleeing from the wrath of his brother, Esau, he had a vision of a ladder reaching from earth to heaven with angels ascending and descending on it. It so stirred Jacob that he wanted to give something to God, but he had gone out empty of anything but the basic provisions necessary for his trip. He covenanted that if God would bless him with material goods, he would pay a tithe back to the Lord. It really was a crafty covenant, for it amounted to a mere 10% commission on what God would provide, but God accepted it. He still does.

There are some Christians who have difficulty accepting the principle of covenanting with God, but God has revealed Himself as a God of covenants. He has consistently offered covenants to us, and has shown Himself throughout the Scriptures to be willing to enter into a covenant we initiate with Him. Oftentimes these covenants are called vows. The one warning we are given about offering God a vow is: "*When you make a vow to God, do not delay in fulfilling it. He has no pleasure in fools; fulfill your vow.*"[41] In other words, don't change the rules after you get what you want.

In Hannah's case, God needed Samuel more than Hannah did. In keeping her vow and returning a spiritually trained son to an ungodly priesthood for the service of the Lord, all Israel was blessed with the godly leadership of Samuel. Who knows what the history of Israel might have been if Hannah had not entered into a covenant with God in prayer.

What is so eloquent about a prayer of covenant? Perhaps it is the desperate cry of a believer priest so aware of his or her need that a covenant is made to obtain an answer. God loves that level of earnest praying. It is a cry from the heart, not merely a communication from the head. It is both a prayer of emotion and devotion. Try it sometime. It works.

Solomon's *Prayer of Dedication*

Before he ever took the throne as king of Israel, Solomon was commissioned by his father, David, to build the temple David had been denied the privilege of building, although he had designed and gathered the materials necessary for its construction. Early in his reign, Solomon told his subjects, "*Behold, I build an house to the name of the LORD my God, to dedicate it to him . . .*"[42] He kept his word, and when this magnificent structure was completed, he prayed one of the outstanding prayers in the Bible as he dedicated this structure to the service of God. His prayer is recorded in 2 Chronicles 6. The purpose was dedicated, the plans were dedicated, and the completed structure was dedicated to God. No one could doubt whose house this was.

In giving the Law, God provided for dedicating things to Himself and His service. Persons could dedicate animals, property, gifts, themselves, and even their children to the service of God. This provision did not cease when the New Testament came into being. The early church dedicated Paul and Silas as missionaries. Men were set aside as deacons and elders in the service of the Lord. Special offerings were dedicated to specific godly purposes.

The prayer of dedication is a love prayer. Almost all religions, Christian and others, have provision for dedicating children. As a pastor, I was delighted to dedicate the offspring of those who attended my church. It was an acknowledgment that all life comes from God and should be given back to Him.

I went a step beyond merely dedicating babies. I used to go into the parking lot to lead members into a prayer of dedication of their latest automobile to God's service. They were merely giving back what God had given to them. I also went to their homes to help them dedicate the building God had allowed them to buy, lease, or rent. I wanted the people to realize that everything we possess is a gift from God and should be available to the service of God.

It is not sufficient that God has given Himself to us. It is imperative that we give ourselves to God. Paul pled, "*Do not offer the parts of your body to sin, as instruments of wickedness, but rather offer yourselves to God, as those who have been brought from death to life; and offer the parts of your body to him as instruments of righteousness.*"[43] Paul was very practical. He did not call for us to merely give God our spirits and souls, he said our entire person should be dedicated to the Lord. He further reminds us, "*You were bought at a price. Therefore honor God with your body.*"[44]

Persons who have been dedicated to God by their parents need to make a personal dedication as they mature. It is primarily a matter of re-consecration. It is an acknowledgment that we have been given to God—we are not our own. When we have praised ourselves into the presence of the Lord and begin to talk to Him in various forms of prayer, we do ourselves a service to remind God that we belong to Him. We can rededicate ourselves to His will while enjoying His presence. It is not so much a submission to a command as it is an impulse of love— but how sweet it sounds to God. It is a prayer of eloquence for us to re-dedicate ourselves and everything we possess to God.

These examples of ways to talk to God when you find yourself in His presence are not exhaustive. They are only illustrative. It should, however, be sufficient to convince us that prayer need not be a vain repetition of requests. Prayer is communication with the most interesting person in the universe—God. Enjoy it; enjoy Him! It is the heritage of a believer priest.

These ten forms of prayer will very likely lead to the highest form of prayer—love talk, but that is the heart of worship and needs a full chapter of its own.

Chapter 7 Endnotes

1. Habakkuk 2:20

2. Jeremiah 33:3, *NIV*

3. 1 Samuel 23:2

4. 1 Samuel 23:10-12

5. Daniel 9:3-4

6. Hebrews 4:12-13, *NIV*

7. Matthew 5:8

8. Jeremiah 10:23-24, *NIV*

9. Romans 8:28, *NIV*

10. Luke 22:42

11. Jeremiah 29:11-13, *NIV*

12. James 4:7

13. Winfield S. Weeden, *I surrender All*, public domain

14. 1 Kings 17:21-22, *NIV*

15. 1 John 5:14, *NIV*

16. Matthew 6:10, *NIV*

17. Philippians 4:6, *NIV*

18. Hebrews 11:6, *NIV*

19. 1 Peter 5:7, *NIV*

20. Deuteronomy 9:25-26, *NIV*

21. John 16:24

22. James 4:2

23. 2 Kings 19:14-15, *NIV*

24. Matthew 12:34

25. Psalm 104:1, *NIV*

26. Ephesians 3:20, *NIV*

27. 2 Peter 3:18, *NIV*

28. Psalm 77:10

29. Ibid

30. Psalm 77:11-13, *NIV*

31. Psalm 46:1, *NIV*
32. William M. Runyan, *Great Is Thy Faithfulness*, 1923. Renewal 1951, Hope Publishing Co.
33. See Jonah 1:17; Matthew 12:40
34. Jonah 2:7, *NIV*
35. Jonah 2:9, *NIV*
36. Acts 27:35
37. Luke 22:19
38. 1 Thessalonians 5:18
39. 1 Samuel 1:11, *NIV*
40. James 1:17, *NIV*
41. Ecclesiastes 5:4, *NIV*
42. 2 Chronicles 2:4
43. Romans 6:13, *NIV*
44. 1 Corinthians 6:20, *NIV*

8
The Efficacy of the Priesthood
The Believer Priest's Worship

Don't stumble over the word *efficacy.* It is merely another form of the word *efficient. Webster's Dictionary* defines it as "effectiveness. The quality or degree of being efficient." Just as not all auto mechanics are equally efficient, so some believer priests function at a very low efficiency rate while others are super efficient in their calling. These priests may be equally qualified, properly trained, and duly set in office, but some fulfill their office much better than others.

God does not seem to look for brilliant persons to become believer priests. He has consistently used very common people as His priests. What He does demand of His priests is obedience to

His Word. This will make them efficient in their work. God's first requirement of a believer priest is, "Do it My way."

In our American world of franchise businesses, there are still failures that end in bankruptcy. Analysis, after the fact, usually reveals that the manager ignored the rules and recommendations of the franchise company and set out to "do it my way," but he or she lacked the expertise to go it alone.

Similarly, God has given us everything we need to be successful believer priests. He has franchised the ministry with ample safeguards against failure, but the rules must be followed for the ministry of a priest to be successful. There is little room for individual entrepreneurship. When the rules are violated, failure is around the corner.

The Priority of Worship for Believer Priests

Some believer priests fulfill their calling with great efficiency, and others repeatedly fail in their mission, although they invest time and energy in the task. The difference is not rooted in personality or preparation. It is found in the priorities that have been set and followed. God's priority has consistently been worship before service. As we have already seen, Jesus attested to this in the wilderness when He told the tempter, "*Get thee hence, Satan: for it is written, Thou shalt worship the Lord thy god, and him only shalt thou serve.*"[1] This order has never changed on earth or in heaven. It remains WORSHIP FIRST; SERVICE SECOND!

This priority seems to be instinctive to the new convert. Having been cleansed from sin and transferred from the kingdom of darkness into the kingdom of light, the inherent reaction of this redeemed person is worship. He or she may not know much about the theology of worship, but the rejoicing in the heart and the freedom in the released soul inspires the spirit to give glory, honor, and praise to the Lord. Worship is as natural to the freshly redeemed person as singing is to the canary.

It is unfortunate that religion so quickly ladens this rejoicing Christian with duties, responsibilities, and "ministries." Somehow older Christians convince the younger Christians that God needs their service. Before long, the ones who had been burdened with sin are burdened with religious activities that crowd out the joyful responses of worship. Of course there is Christian service to be done, but it should never replace worship. It should flow out of worship.

It is self-evident that the best Christian service comes as a flow of the Holy Spirit through the lives of believers. This flow comes during worship. It is a by-product of being with Jesus. How can we know what He wants us to do if we have not been in His presence to hear His voice?

Furthermore, the strongest motivation for service is not projected guilt, but divine love. When we have been in a love mode in the presence of Jesus, we are motivated to anything and everything He wants done. Love duties never seem like work. They become visible demonstrations of our love for Jesus.

It is likely that most believer priests intuitively know that worship of God should precede service for God, but actually following that order is difficult. Worship requires us to contact God in the spiritual realm about which we know very little. There seems to be little ritual that brings us into God's presence so we can worship. The way we made contact yesterday may not make contact today. True worship requires experimentation and variety. Most of us don't feel that we have time for this.

Furthermore, the insistent needs and demands of life are very present. Have you ever set aside a time for prayer and seeking God when the phone did not ring, the children did not call for you, or someone knocked on your front door? Life around us does not remain passive. It is constantly active. Voices call to us from radios, television sets, computers, and compact disks. There is visual stimulation calling for our attention in newspapers, magazines, billboards, and direct mail advertising. Whether vocal or visual, the world is demanding our attention and requesting our service. In contrast to this, God's voice seems muted and distant.

Ministering to needs and Christian service is often little more than reaction to pressing circumstances. Worship, on the other hand, demands disciplined action. We must take the initiative to worship. It forces us to close the door to life's whirling activities and get alone and be quiet with God. Through the ages, men and women who have exercised this discipline have found an inner peace that enables them to face their God in a way no textbook could unfold Him to them. Most of them became outstanding servants of God, but for the most part, they ministered **with** God rather than **for** God.

Roxanne Brant wrote:

> One of the main reasons for the power failure today in the Christian Church is that Christians have failed to minister to the Lord. Biblically the evidence is that our ministry to the Lord must come before our ministry to men if we are to be effective. Even after being filled with the Holy Spirit, if our priorities regarding these two types of ministry are reversed, we will be helpless and impotent before the heathen world. We need to once again dig down into the springs of God's life and bury ourselves in Him, the Source. We need to be caught up in the wonder of the person of Jesus Christ of Nazareth, to know Him intimately and deeply: then we will find that our ministry God-ward will urge us man-ward with a new freshness and power, and then we will not only talk of God's power, but will also see it demonstrated.[2]

God's divine order of *worship first, service second,* is more for our sakes than for God's sake. We need God far more than we need another activity in life. We need the pure motivation for service that worship provides. We need the direction in our Christian service that comes only from God. We need the inner peace and quietness that energizes Christian service, and we need a true knowledge of God more than we need an academic knowledge of the doctrine of God. All of this is a natural by-product of being in God's presence in worship.

David Watson wrote, "Evangelical or social activities can never be a substitute for this worship. If we neglect our foremost calling, we become spiritually arid in ourselves. We have nothing of lasting value to offer the world and we dishonor God."[3] Many full-time Christian workers have learned this the hard way.

If we are to function under God's franchise as believer priests, we had better follow the written priorities—worship first; service second. It is a prerequisite for success. J. Oswald Sanders warns, "We should not separate what God has joined. Worship is no substitute for service, nor is service a substitute for worship, but true worship must always be expressed in loving service."[4]

The Persons of Worship

When God called His people out of Egypt, He told them, "*Ye shall be unto me a kingdom of priests, and an holy nation.*"[5] God's initial desire was to have all Israel be a kingdom of priests unto Himself. It was a high and holy calling, but it was given to persons who were unholy and who had lived the low life of slaves for 400 plus years. They weren't ready for such a call. Their generations of slavery had produced a resentment of authority and a hatred of authority figures. Their position had been changed by the divine exodus, but their passions had not.

During their wandering in the wilderness, their eight major rebellions against God and His leaders evidences deep resentment against authority figures. How could they truly worship God when they resented Him, His ways, His provision, and His leadership? They, as we, had to learn obedient submission before they could openly worship God.

Because of their incapacities, God chose Aaron and his sons to become the priesthood for Israel, and then after the disobedience of two of the sons, God gave the entire tribe of Levi as assistants to these priests. These became the representative worshipers of Jehovah, and through the ordinances God appointed, they gently led individuals into worship of Jehovah.

The history of Israel establishes that the observance of rituals and ordinances did not produce much change in the lives of the people. The cry of the prophets was for a return to the worship of Jehovah, but the people seemed set on self-worship and the worship of idols. They had a worshiping nature, but they did not have a surrendered nature to Jehovah. They consistently looked for other gods and credited their deliverance and provisions to them. Human nature hasn't changed very much, has it?

It is not until the finished work of the Cross was made available through the shed blood of Jesus that our soul/spirits could be purged from sin and selfishness and made pliable to the will of God. It is the redeemed who have the capacity to function as believer priests.

The apostle Peter wrote: "*But ye are a chosen generation, a royal priesthood, an holy nation, a peculiar people; that ye should show forth the praises of him who hath called you out of darkness into his marvellous light.*"[6] What Israel could not rise to fulfill, God has made available to His Church, comprised of Jews and Gentiles. It works because God, by His Spirit, affects the necessary changes in us that enable us to function as believer priests. The stated purpose of His choice and appointment to the priesthood is "*that ye should show forth the praises of Him who hath called you. . . .*" We have been chosen and changed to become worshipers of God.

Twice the book of Revelation says that God "*hath made us kings and priests unto God and his Father; to him be glory and dominion for ever and ever. Amen.*"[7] Modern speech translations prefer to translate the Greek as "*kingdom and priests*" or "*kingdom of priests.*" This was God's original plan for His people. The people may have changed, but God's plan hasn't. Israel didn't seem to be ready for this holy distinction, so God sent His Son into the world to make change so available that New Testament believers are qualified (by His action) to function as worshiping priests.

God doesn't need priests to offer sacrifices. Jesus was the final holocaust offering. God's offer of the priesthood to individual believers is to release an anthem of worship that would echo around the world. We need not go to some "holy city" to worship. God has worshiping priests throughout the world. It becomes a holy place wherever His Holy Spirit is released in a worship mode, whether that worship flows from an individual or a collective body of believers.

The Performance of Worship

In the Old Testament priesthood, worship involved dedicated places, special garments, divinely appointed ritual, and abundant sacrifice offerings. In the New Testament, these have all been forsaken as a building leaves its foundations. Ritual has given way to reality. Shadows have been replaced with substance. While the Old Testament rituals pointed to Christ, New Testament worship is personally involved with Christ.

This is beautifully illustrated in the intimate worship Mary performed with Jesus when she washed His feet with her tears and dried them with her hair. Then she broke the alabaster box she had brought with her and poured the liquid nard on Christ's head and feet. No one in the room could deny that she was worshiping Jesus. Although some considered the pouring of the spikenard a waste, neither she nor Jesus saw it as outlandishly extravagant.[8]

There were many persons in the room and some of them were admirers of Jesus. Still it was Mary who became the worshiper, and her act of worship teaches us several things about worship.

First, worship is very personal. It was not done by public proclamation. It was a private, personal gift of love to Jesus. She did not need the services of another priest—she poured out the tears and fragrant oil personally. One wonders if "public worship" might be a misnomer. We may be with other people when we worship, but true worship is an intimate contact between one person and Jesus.

A second segment of worship Mary's act illustrates is that worship is very costly. Judas quickly estimated the value at 300 pence, a full year's salary for a workingman at that time. Mary may have been saving this for her burial or perhaps as a dowry for marriage. Whatever value it was to Mary, it seemed to be the best expression of worship unto the Jesus who had done so much for her in restoring her brother Lazarus from the dead.

Still a third principle of worship illustrated in this story of Mary is that true worship will always be accepted by Jesus. To the critics, Jesus said, "*Verily I say unto you, Wheresoever this gospel shall be preached in the whole world, there shall also this, that this woman hath done, be told for a memorial of her.*"[9] Others may not have understood, but Jesus did. Onlookers are often critical of our worship expressions, but as long as they come from a pure heart, they are always accepted by Jesus and they are long remembered.

A fourth factor that applies in worship is the matter of reciprocity. As Mary transferred the fragrant oil from Christ's head to His feet and wiped the excess with her hair, she took on the same fragrance that Jesus now wore. When we worship, we come out of God's presence smelling just like Jesus.

Far too often, we merely banquet with Jesus and His friends and don't worship Him. When we leave, we may smell like food and friends, but we don't have the heavenly fragrance on us. John Henry Howett wrote:

> We leave our places of worship, and no deep and inexpressible wonder sits upon our faces—when we get out into the streets our faces are one with the faces of those who have left the theaters and music halls. There is nothing about us to suggest that we've been looking at anything stupendous and overwhelming. Far back in my boyhood I remember an old saint telling me that after some services he liked to make his way home alone by quiet by-paths, so that the hush of the Almighty might remain on his awed and prostrate soul. That is the element we are losing.[10]

The psalmist testified, "*I will sing unto the LORD as long as I live: I will sing praise to my God while I have my being. My meditation of him shall be sweet: I will be glad in the LORD.*" The psalm ends in verse 35 with the injunction, "*Bless thou the LORD, O my soul. Praise ye the LORD.*"[11] That is what worship is all about—blessing the Lord, not seeking a blessing from the Lord.

John MacArthur, Jr. asks:

> Why do you go to church? when you meet together with the saints,is it really for worship? or do you go to church for what you can get out of it? Do you come away having scrutinized the soloist, analyzed the choir, and criticized the message? . . . even if you go to church selfishly to seek a blessing, you have missed the point of worship. We go to give glory, not to get blessed. An understanding of that will affect how you critique the church experience. The issue isn't, 'Did I get anything out of it?,' but, 'Did I from my heart give glory to God?' Since blessing comes from God in response to worship, if you aren't blessed, it isn't usually because of poor music or preaching (though there may occasionally prove to be insurmountable obstacles), but because of a selfish heart that does not give glory to God.[12]

The Believer Priest Worships in His Spirit

As Jesus put it, "*But the hour cometh, and now is, when the true worshippers shall worship the Father in spirit and in truth: for the Father seeketh such to worship him. God is a Spirit: and they that worship him must worship him in spirit and in truth.*"[13] The Koine Greek of the New Testament offers but one word for "spirit"—*pneuma*. It sometimes refers to the human spirit, sometimes the Holy Spirit, and is even translated angel. The translators are very dependent upon the context to know whether the writer refers to the Spirit of God, in which case they usually capitalize the word Spirit, or whether it refers to the human spirit, in which case they use a lower case "s".

There is a difference of opinion among translators as to whether these words of Jesus refer to the spirit of persons or the Spirit of God. Either way it gives us a broader understanding of worship. Let's assume that Jesus meant the human spirit. If that is so, He said that worship of God transpires in the spirit of man. This is absolutely accurate. He had just affirmed that God is Spirit. If we are to commune and communicate with Him, we will have to do so in our spirits, for like calls to to like.

As we'll see in a moment, worship may be expressed in our soul and with our body, but it actually takes place in our spirit—the eternal portion of our being. How careful we must be lest we mistake feelings as worship rather than use them as an expression of that worship. It is possible for art, music, and even memory to induce worshipful attitudes and feelings, but if true worship occurs, it will not be in the intellect or the soul—it must be in the spirit.

Believer priests need to be in touch with their spirits. It is not only the eternal part of our nature, it is where the Holy Spirit resides. It is that part of us with which Jesus communicates, and is where all revelation from God comes. It is the human channel that transmits worship unto Almighty God.

The Believer Priest Worships in the Holy Spirit

If Jesus meant to convey the truth that worship must be in "the Holy Spirit," He was equally accurate, for true worship apart from the Holy Spirit is impossible. Surely "*the true worshippers shall worship the Father in* [the Holy] *Spirit and in truth*."[14] How else could we really worship God? We know nothing about God except what the Holy Spirit has revealed to us. Similarly, we know nothing of true worship except when the Holy Spirit flows it through us. To worship the true God in truth requires the unction of the Holy Spirit.

Roxanne Brant said:

> We must move beyond the limitations of the heart and person and into the limitless dimension of the Holy Spirit if our worship is to be pleasing to God. Set aside an inviolable time each day when you can come apart to minister to Him. Do not retire for the night until you have ministered to Him, until you have performed your priestly function.[15]

Paul wrote: "*For we are the circumcision, which worship God in the spirit, and rejoice in Christ Jesus, and have no confidence in the flesh*."[16] Circumcision refers to a covenant relationship initiated by God for Old Testament believers. Paul told the New

Testament Gentile believers that God's covenant with us is to worship in the Spirit. We who worship in the Spirit are God's covenant people. This verse also says that worship in the Holy Spirit will be a rejoicing worship that exalts Jesus to where fleshly pride and self-confidence melt in dependence upon the Lord.

We dare not take the space to enlarge upon the role of the Holy Spirit in our worship. Suffice it to say that He is the inspiration for, the instigator of, the instructor in, and interpreter of our worship. Worship without Him is somewhat like trying to shop in a foreign country when we have no knowledge of the language or customs of the people. We can make gestures and sounds, but we can't do much business. We've all been in "worship" services that were just about that ineffective.

The Believer Priest Worships in Song

The place of the believer priest's worship is in his spirit by action of the Holy Spirit, but the means of expressing that worship to God are varied. Paramount in these expressions of inward devotion and love is singing. How often has our spirit soared into the presence of God on the wings of song, for singing releases both the intellect and the emotions.

David knew that well. From the pasture as he tended sheep to the palace where he led a growing nation, David sang his worship to God. He not only sang songs to the Lord, he wrote worship songs and taught others to sing them. He trained choirs to sing before the Lord every hour of the day to the accompaniment of appointed orchestras. He invented and manufactured musical instruments to be used in the worship of Jehovah. To this godly king, music and worship belonged together like bread and butter.

This singing worship became a vibrant part of the early church's worship. W. E. Vine tells us:

> Christian song did not break forth upon a world which had been hitherto dumb and in which hymns were unknown. The Church was cradled in Judaism and borrowed many of its forms of worship from the temple

> and synagogue. Antiphonal singing goes back to the pre-exilic period of Jewish history (Exodus 15:21; Numbers 10:35 ; 12:17; 1 Samuel 18:7).[17]

"[Martin] Luther recognized the effectiveness of music. He asked 'Why should the devil have all the good music?' and said, 'The substance of true worship is this: that our dear Lord speaks with us through His holy Word, and we in return speak with Him through prayer and songs of praise.'"[18]

That last phrase is the secret to worshiping in song. Luther said, "We in return *speak with Him* through prayer and songs of praise." If what we are singing does not speak to God, it probably is not worship. It is difficult to worship Almighty God while singing about our puny selves. Songs of testimony may bring us to praise, but God needs to be the subject of a song that brings us to worship. So many of today's choruses sing of revival, wind, fire, etc., but where are the songs that sing of God? Where are the old hymns that taught us about God and helped us respond to Him? Is it possible that only a person who really knows God can write a hymn about Him?

Dave Topp reminds us of another factor of using songs in worship. He writes: "God may—react negatively to our worship music when the words we sing do not harmonize with the lives we lead."[19] Unless the song we sing is an honest expression of the life we live, we are merely "whistling in the dark." The music we sing in worship cannot be a substitute for devotion; it must be an expression of it.

Anne Murchison reminds us:

> For those who think they cannot sing, and for those who really cannot sing, the word of God says, 'Make a joyful noise unto the Lord.' We praise and worship in obedience to a spiritual principle that is eternal. We do not do it to please ourselves or others. We do it to please God and therefore fulfill ourselves. When one becomes lost in the wonder of God, one is no longer aware of fleshly inadequacies, but is focused upon the majesty and wonder of God. That is where our focus belongs.[20]

You do not need a trained voice to sing your worship unto God. God is listening to our heart, not our mouth.

The Believer Priest Worships with Love Talk

When we recognize that worship is basically love responding to love, we realize that the speech of commerce will not communicate the inner feelings of love. Frankly, the language of theology seldom describes the inner emotion of the soul/spirit when in the presence of God. Worship needs the language of love.

When young lovers are together, they may begin their conversation about facts, but very quickly they shift to talking about feelings. They use poetic expressions, analogies, comparisons, and exaggerations. When he tells her, "You're the most beautiful woman in the world," she interprets it to mean, "I have intense feelings of love for you." She knows it is not factual—it is feeling, but she loves it.

Solomon's *Song of Songs* is a beautiful example of love talk. He speaks of the object of his affections with tenderness. He extols her eyes, teeth, hair, and dress. She, in turn, compares him to a lily of the field and a tree of the field. Poetically, they are expressing love feelings they have one for another.

This is a wonderful way to express worship to God. Tell Him the way you feel about Him. You may be surprised to learn that your feelings and your theology are not in total agreement. What we have been taught about God and what we have discovered Him to be through worship often conflict. Don't let your head overrule your heart. God is infinitely more wonderful and glorious than words can ever express. He, the Person, is far greater than any performance He has ever done.

We know that lovers exaggerate when talking love talk. Do we dare exaggerate when talking to God? Frankly, it is impossible to speak beyond the truth of God. He is infinitely more wonderful and glorious than we have yet experienced. After we have stretched our imaginations to the breaking point, we have not yet exhausted the merits of our Lord. Even in the matter of comprehending the works of God, Paul had to admit: "*No eye has seen, no ear has heard, no mind has conceived what God has prepared for those who love him.*"[21] If we cannot even imagine all God has prepared for us, what chance have we of really knowing all that God is? Go ahead and exaggerate. Imagination is the first step in faith anyhow.

Our worship will, of necessity, be limited by our concept of God. In our love communication with Him, we enlarge our comprehension of God. We may not know the increased facts, but we know the increased love we feel, and that becomes a platform for further revelation of the goodness of our God.

Most people initially find it awkward to speak love talk to God. Men generally find it more difficult than women, for women are usually more in touch with their feelings than are men. After the early embarrassment wears off, however, both men and women find a release in their spirits toward God that releases deep emotions of love and adoration when they talk the language of love to God. It is a doorway to a closer relationship with God.

When you speak love talk to God, you will hear Him speak love talk to you, and that will motivate you to higher worship and greater service. James D. Robertson reminds us, "It is the worship experience that charges the soul with the dynamic of God's presence, inspiring total response; and that invests the commonplace with a light that never was seen on land or sea" [22]

A good beginning in this form of worship expression would be to read Solomon's Song of Songs aloud; maybe while kneeling before the Lord. This would give you a tailor-made vocabulary, plus the assurance that since you are quoting God's Word back to God, there can be nothing wrong with what you are saying.

The Believer Priest Worships in His Emotions

Emil G. Hirsch reminds us, "The poetry of the soul . . . has . . . moments when the poetic expression rises spontaneously to the lips. This has been the weakness of rationalism, that it neglected to take into account the soul of man."[23] Worship deeply involves the soul, for that is the seat of intellect and emotion. God doesn't want us to leave our mind and emotions in bed when we rise to worship Him.

Mindless, unfeeling worship is totally unacceptable to God and it is useless to us.

William Temple wrote:

> Worship is the submission of all our nature to God. It is the quickening of conscience by His holiness; the nourishment of mind with His truth, the purifying of imagination by His beauty; the opening of the heart to His love; the surrender of will to His purpose and all this gathered up in adoration, the most selfless emotion of which our nature is capable and, therefore, the chief remedy for that self-centeredness, which is our original sin and the source of all actual sin.[24]

Jesus said it far more succinctly when He quoted the Old Testament proclamation: "*Thou shalt love the Lord thy God with all thy heart, and with all thy soul, and with all thy mind. This is the first and great commandment.*"[25] Love requires both intellect and emotion. Worship ("*Love the Lord thy God*") demands the full expression of both of these faculties of our being ("*with all*").

The application of the intellect to worship doesn't seem to bother people—it is expected. It is when the human emotions get involved in our worship that some people become critical. They are like King David's wife, Michal, who seriously criticized David for his display of emotion when he returned the Ark of the Covenant to Jerusalem.[26] It is probable that Michal remembered the extreme display of emotions her father had shown when among the prophets. She transferred this unbridled behavior to David's intense worship as he danced before the Lord. So can we. Most of us have witnessed at least one instance of extreme religious behavior in church. We need to be careful lest the extreme display of another produces in us such negative reactions as to push us in the opposite direction. Being stoic will not balance out another person's exuberant behavior.

John MacArthur, Jr. reminds us that:

> Worship is not giddy. It does not rush into God's presence unprepared and insensitive to His majesty. It

> is not shallow, superficial, or flippant. Worship is life lived in the presence of an infinitely righteous and omnipresent God by one utterly aware of His holiness and consequently overwhelmed with his own unholiness.[27]

While I totally agree with this statement, I would like to say that worship is not stoic either. I have been in many "worship" services that were so impassive and unimpassioned that I wondered if I had stumbled into a classroom of algebra students. We are not trying to understand God in our worship, for Paul taught us, "*O the depth of the riches both of the wisdom and knowledge of God! how unsearchable are his judgments, and his ways past finding out!*"[28] When we worship, we are relating to a living person far above us who has stooped to let us hug His neck. If worship is, as I contend, love responding to love, it cannot be done dispassionately. Love received quickens the emotions as well as the mind.

Rather than use their emotions as servants, some persons so suppress them as to live a colorless existence. Anne Murchison wrote:

> If you are mired in a pit of emotions and have never found the proper place to give of yourself emotionally, praise and worship are the vehicles necessary in your life. If you have been locked into a prison without access to feelings and emotions, praise and worship are the vehicles necessary for liberty in this area of your life. There is no love life that flourishes without feeling and emotion. There is no pleasure that can be fully enjoyed without giving expression to it.[29]

Tears Are An Acceptable Expression of Worship

Being near Jesus in times of worship inevitably brings tears to my eyes. We sometimes forget that we do not cry only when we are sad. Great emotions of joy also trigger tears. Just watch a mother embrace her child who has been lost, or closely observe the winner of a sporting event. Their unbridled joy overflows into tears. Why, then, should we not cry while worshiping the Redeemer and Restorer of our life? It can be evidence of an effervescent inner joy.

Someone has wisely said that, "Tears are a language to God." He understands our tears whether they are motivated by sadness or joy. Don't choke them back. He reads them perfectly.

Tears also release pent-up emotions deep in our spirit. Sometimes what our lips cannot say, our tears say eloquently. Tears can be a worship expression of great depth and feeling. Release them.

Laughter Is An Acceptable Expression of Worship

Laughter is a marvelous channel for the release of emotion. Skilled speakers have learned to use this as a tool to unlock an audience. Religion often suppresses laughter as being "unGodlike" in times of worship, but God actually has a wonderful sense of humor. Just look around you the next time you are in church. If God lacks a sense of humor, how can He stand being around us? The unbridled joy that nearness to God can induce often must break out in laughter or rupture a person.

I know that worship is a serious activity, but we should take God seriously, not ourselves. If we function naturally in worship as we do in other life situations, we will have times of laughter. Don't bury your face in your handkerchief while stifling a good laugh. Roar out your joy to Jesus.

Jesus calls us children and one of the characteristics of children is their ability to spontaneously break into laughter so easily. What's wrong with a happy giggle in God's presence?

Body Movement Is An Acceptable Expression of Worship

Many of us were raised to believe that standing rigidly at attention is the proper way of worshiping God. If we are at a funeral this is acceptable behavior, but when we are in a worship service, we need to release our bodies to express our feelings. In conversation with one another, we use our bodies to accentuate our speech. We nod our head, move our arms, shift our feet, and wink our eye. If this is natural expression to us, and it is, shouldn't it be used when we are communicating the most important message of our lives—worship?

The raising of the hands, clapping, waving our arms, and even dancing have always been a part of jubilant worship. While our actions should not disturb the comfort of those around us, we dare not so suppress our physical language as to try to release our worshipful feelings with words alone. We lack the capacity to excel at this. Be yourself! God made you that way, and He is never shocked when you express yourself honestly.

Worship Is An Attitude

Quite obviously, then, worship is more than an attitude; it is an attitude expressed, and the magnitude of the attitude determines the measure of the actions. A lukewarm heart cannot perform boiling hot worship, nor can a rebellious life revere God with any depth of sincerity. Conversely, boiling hot worship cannot be confined to two hymns and a prayer. It will boil with emotion and scream for channels of expression. Unless we have something in our life that disqualifies us from the priesthood, our worship will be vibrant, vocal, emotional, and physical. That's the way God made us.

Chapter 8 Endnotes

1. Matthew 4:10

2. Roxanne Brant, *Ministering to the Lord*, Florida, Roxanne Brant Crusades, 1973, p. 7

3. David Watson, *I Believe in the Church*, Grand Rapids, Wm. B. Eerdmans, 1978, p. 179

4. J. Oswald Sanders, *Enjoying Intimacy With God*, Chicago, Moody Press, 1980, p. 29

5. Exodus 19:6

6. 1 Peter 2:9

7. Revelation 1:6, Revelation 5:10

8. See John 12:1-8

9. Matthew 26:13

10. John Henry Howett, *The Transfigured Church*, London, James Clark and Co., 1910, p. 22

11. Psalm 104:33-35

12. John MacArthur, Jr., *The Ultimate Priority*, Chicago, Moody Bible Institute, 1983, p. 13

13. John 4:23-24

14. John 4:23

15. Roxanne Brant, *From Decision to Discipleship*, Missouri, Impact books, 1974, p. 29

16. Philippians 3:3

17. W. E. Vine, *Expository Dictionary of the New Testament, II*, London, Oliphants, 1970, p. 18

18. Gunnar Urang, *Church Music and the Glory of God*, Illinois, Christian Service Foundation, 1956, p. 1

19. Dave Topp, *Music in the Christian Community*, Grand Rapids, Wm. B. Eerdmans, 1976, p. 15

20. Anne Murchison, *Praise and Worship in Earth As It Is in Heaven*, Waco, Word Books, 1981, p. 132

21. 1 Corinthians 2:9, *NIV*

22. James D. Robertson, *Ministers Worship Handbook*, Grand Rapids, Baker Book House, 1974, p. 15

23. Emil G. Hirsch, *My Religion*, New York, The MacMillan Co., 1925, p. 119

24. William Temple, *Reading in St. John's Gospel*, New York, MacMillan, 1939, p. 68

25. Matthew 22:37-38, Deuteronomy 6:5

26. 2 Samuel 6:15-23

27. John MacArthur, Jr., *The Ultimate Priority*, Chicago, Moody Bible Institute, 1963, p. 13

28. Romans 11:33

29. Anne Murchison, *Praise and Worship in Earth As It Is in Heaven*, Waco, Word Books, 1981, p. 132

9
The Exclusions to the Priesthood
The Believer Priest's Disqualification

Life has taught us that there is often a distinct difference between provision and possession. Even in Christian living, God's promised provision and positions are often far above the level of performance in many believers' lives.

The problem cannot be with God, for He is no respecter of persons,[1] nor does He withdraw something He has offered. If a believer is not functioning as a priest unto God, it is not God's fault. Provisionally, "*He hast made us . . . priests.*"[2] God's provision is always secure—God's Word guarantees this to us, and God's Word never fails.

So why are some believers possessors of what to others is but a promise? A fairly common scapegoat we blame for this is the devil. Some people seem to feel that unless they have Satan's permission, they cannot live in God's provision or successfully function as a believer priest. Unwittingly they have made the devil bigger than God. Since when does God need the permission of anybody to do what He wants?

There is no doubt that all callings of God will be challenged here on earth. The devil is "*the accuser of our brethren,*"[3] and he is very good at it. Good, but unsuccessful at defeating God's appointments. The visionary prophet Zechariah saw Joshua standing before the Lord in heaven. Alongside Joshua stood Satan making repeated accusations against this priest. The LORD rebuked Satan, stripped the priest of his filthy garments, and clothed Joshua with a divine garment of righteousness. Case closed![4] Satan's accusations are always unacceptable in Heaven's court, for Jesus said that the devil is a proven liar and the father of lies.[5]

The devil might like to get us impeached, but he lacks the clout to do so. If God has appointed us to the priesthood, hell cannot disannul that appointment.

If we begin to do a credible job as believer priests, we can probably expect an attack from another source. It was certainly true for Aaron the High Priest. During the wilderness wanderings, Korah led a group of 250 men in an insurrection against the Aaronic priesthood.[6] Korah presented himself as more qualified to be the High Priest than was Aaron. After all, unlike Aaron, he had never built a golden calf and led Israel in worshiping it as the god that had brought them out of Egypt.

God instructed Moses to have each challenger bring his rod and, with Aaron's rod, they were laid before the Lord in the Holy of Holies. God said that the rod that budded would indicate the divine choice for High Priest. In the morning when the rods were brought out to be examined, all rods had withered and died except the rod of Aaron. His had not only budded, it bore blossoms and produced ripe almonds. God proved that He does not always choose the most qualified persons, but that He qualifies each person He chooses. God not only stands behind His choices; He stands behind the person He chooses. Paul asks, "*If God be for us, who can be against us?*[7]

We will seldom step into a God-given ministry without someone rising up to declare a greater ability to serve. Sometimes this insurrection is strong, well-organized, and armed with disturbing facts. We know who is ultimately behind such actions. How cleverly the devil hides behind the human ego and manipulates an insurrection, and how decisively God reaffirms His choice.

No, we cannot say the devil, demons, or other people keep us from fulfilling God's call on our lives. If we are still talking promise while others are enjoying position, the problem must rest in us. There must be something in us that disqualifies us from service.

Availability and Desire Do Not Guarantee Appointment

Tina, my youngest daughter, was one of thirty-five candidates who submitted to rigorous training for the job of telephone consultant for a major health organization. These applicants trained for three months, but only three of them were hired. My daughter, who was not only hired, but subsequently was made an instructor, says that this attrition rate is quite normal. Many more persons are available and have initial requirements than are capable of functioning satisfactorily in the pressure of this type of work. Willingness and availability are a small part of qualification. There are many other factors that can best be determined during on-the-job training.

This is true of the priesthood. It is great to be available and desirous, but this is not necessarily sufficient. In the Old Testament economy, all male children born to the tribe of Levi were candidates for the priesthood. They had passed the first qualification in that birth.

Similarly, every born again Christian is a candidate to become a believer priest. This has been the underlying theme of this book. We have been made "*A royal priesthood*" [8] by action and edict of Jesus Christ. Satan does not have sufficient power or authority to withstand this appointment. Positionally, we are born to the priesthood. It is our destiny!

Still, it doesn't require a census taker to reveal that not all Christians function in the believer priesthood. Something, other than satanic opposition, seems to have disqualified many believers from serving their God and their fellow believers in spiritual service. Like the applicants with my daughter, "*Many are called, but few are chosen.*" [9]

God has requirements and minimum standards for His priests. The Levite priests in the days of Moses discovered this. These men had not only been born to the priesthood, their parents had held this office up in front of their faces from the day of their circumcision. Their boyhood was lived in anticipation of being a priest. Very likely their childhood games mimicked whatever role their fathers played in their priestly functions. In the day when a trade was passed from father to son, it was the priests who instilled the earliest training for priesthood in their children.

When these young men were about 25 years old, they began their formal training for the priesthood. The older, "retired" priests were the instructors. Much of this training was "hands-on" training. These men become interns to the priesthood.

There must have been a great deal to learn, for they could not be consecrated to the priesthood until they were 30 years of age—the age a Jewish boy was declared to be a man. How they must have anticipated being appointed to the priesthood during this five year internship. Once they were hallowed to the priesthood, they would serve 20 years. Then at age 50, they would retire from active service and instruct the younger intern priests.

Training and Talent Do Not Guarantee Appointment

According to Exodus 29, this anticipated consecration was a seven-day ritual that began by being brought into the Outer Court where they were stripped and washed with water. While this was ceremonious, it was also practical. It gave the High Priest an opportunity to assess the physical qualifications or disqualifications of the candidate, for even though the candidate had been born to the right family and trained properly, he still had to meet certain physical qualifications.

God told Moses, "*Speak unto Aaron, saying, Whosoever he be of thy seed in their generations that hath any blemish, let him not approach to offer the bread of his God.*"[10] In the verses that follow, God lists twelve physical blemishes or "defects" as the New International Version translates it, that would disqualify the individual from priestly service. God said:

> *For whatsoever man he be that hath a blemish, he shall not approach: (1) a blind man, or (2) a lame, or he that hath a (3) flat nose, or (4) any thing superfluous, Or a man that is (5) broken-footed, or (6) brokenhanded, (7) Or crookbacked, or (8) a dwarf, or that hath (9) a blemish in his eye, or (10) be scurvy, or (11) scabbed, or hath (12) his stones broken; No man that hath a blemish of the seed of Aaron the priest shall come nigh to offer the offerings of the LORD made by fire: he hath a blemish; he shall not come nigh to offer the bread of his God. He shall eat the bread of his God, both of the most holy, and of the holy. Only he shall not go in unto the veil, nor come nigh unto the altar, because he hath a blemish; that he profane not my sanctuaries: for I the LORD do sanctify them.*[11]

Wouldn't this have been self-evident? Did Aaron need these guidelines or were they written for New Testament believers? Remember Paul wrote: "*These things happened to them as examples and were written down as warnings for us, on whom the fulfillment of the ages has come.*"[12] Isn't it likely that these physical disqualifications are types or pictures of spiritual conditions that disqualify believer priests from serving God?

A Spiritually Blind Person Is Disqualified From Serving As A Priest

The first defect to disqualify a priest from serving was blindness. How could a blind man serve as a priest? Yet this blind person had served a five year's apprenticeship successfully. It is likely that he depended heavily upon his fellow students. He had to be led and walked through each operation. He found it very difficult to function independently. Peter may have had this in mind when he exhorted believers:

> *And beside this, giving all diligence, add to your faith virtue; and to virtue knowledge; And to knowledge temperance; and to temperance patience; and to patience godliness; And to godliness brotherly kindness; and to brotherly kindness charity. For if these things be in you, and abound, they make you that ye shall neither be barren nor unfruitful in the knowledge of our Lord Jesus Christ.* ***But he that lacketh these things is blind,*** *and cannot see afar off, and hath forgotten that he was purged from his old sins.*[13]

In my pre-teen and early teen years, I worked with a blind piano tuner. I never got over my amazement at the way he could function in spite of his blindness. He had so tuned his other senses to make up for sightlessness as to be almost eerie. He heard things I did not hear. He had memorized the footsteps of persons like I memorized facial features. I remember that after leaving for college for a year, I walked up to him on a lawn at a campmeeting during summer vacation. He turned my way and said, "Judson, it's so good to see you again." I was amazed.

He was so self-sufficient that he needed me only when we were in unfamiliar places. He used me to guide him to the piano and to tell him the brand name so he would know how to dismantle it for repairs. From there on, I really wasn't important to him.

Many believers are like this. They are truly spiritually blind, but they can function quite well as long as they are in familiar places. Just don't expect them to move into anything new.

This is sad enough in an individual believer, but it is dangerous when that individual is a leader in the things of God—a priest. He must forever be locked into the old familiar ways of God. He cannot see anything new or different and will inherently be afraid of any change. Merely moving the furniture becomes a threat to him.

Like an aging gentleman who can vividly recall his childhood, but can't remember anything that happened yesterday, some believer priests are forever caught up in "the good old days." They recall and function sufficiently in past training, but they are insufficient for present truth or application.

Jesus so succinctly said of the Pharisees of His day, "*Let them alone: they be blind leaders of the blind. And if the blind lead the blind, both shall fall into the ditch.*"[14] We have repeatedly witnessed this tragedy in Christian circles. The unseeing have led the unknowing into ditches.

You may be aware that every miracle Jesus did had been performed through someone in the Old Testament except one—healing blind eyes. Amazingly, the four gospels record more incidents of Christ healing blind eyes than any other form of healing.

Surely this should speak to us spiritually. The Lord doesn't want any of His children to walk blindly. He is the restorer of sight—the giver of light—the one who opens our understanding of divine truth. The wise man wrote: "*The hearing ear, and the seeing eye, the LORD hath made even both of them.*"[15] God is the giver of sight. It isSatan who blinds spiritual vision.[16]

In spiritual application of this Old Testament code, I do not suggest that it refers to a birth defect. Jesus told Nicodemus, "*I tell you the truth, no one can see the kingdom of God unless he is born again.*"[17] The context affirms that Jesus was saying that spiritual vision comes with new birth. When we are saved, we see Jesus. We may not know how to understand other things we see, but our eyes are opened and we are ready for spiritual understanding to come as we learn the things of God.

If none are born blind in God's kingdom, how is it that some become blind? The apostle Paul gives us a couple of clues in his letter to the Corinthian church. He wrote: *"In whom the god of this world hath blinded the minds of them which believe not, lest the light of the glorious gospel of Christ, who is the image of God, should shine unto them."*[18]

Paul first suggests that Satan successfully blinds the minds of some. Sometimes even believers spend too much time looking into the wrong things and lose their spiritual vision. It is obvious that delving into the satanic realm can blind our eyes to the things of God, but it is less obvious that too much looking at the things of Satan's kingdom—the natural world—can diminish and distort our spiritual vision. Some believers called to the priesthood can tell you more about baseball scores, weather reports, and television programs than they can tell you of God's Word. The mind focuses on what the eyes see. As John put it, "*That which we have seen and heard declare we unto you.*"[19] While we are strongly focused on one thing, we may be blind to many other things. The priest who will not fix his vision on the things of God is effectively blind. He or she may know golf, cars, stock market quotes, and the latest neighborhood gossip, but not know God.

In this verse, Paul also suggests that unbelief can cause spiritual blindness—"*which believe not.*" Unbelief causes the mind to disregard what it sees. Jesus said:

> *And in them is fulfilled the prophecy of Esaias, which saith, By hearing ye shall hear, and shall not understand; and seeing ye shall see, and shall not perceive: For this people's heart is waxed gross, and their ears are dull of hearing, and their eyes they have closed; lest at any time they should see with their eyes and hear with their ears, and should understand with their heart, and should be converted, and I should heal*

them. But blessed are your eyes, for they see: and your ears, for they hear.[20]

This willful blindness—the refusal to believe what is seen—is a dangerous form of blindness. This vision is not faulty, but the processing of what is seen is. How often we read into the Bible what we have been taught or what we believe instead of letting God's Word speak for itself. Such blindness has caused thousands of Christians to reject fresh revelations of God. They are willfully blind because of unbelief.

We might also suppose that some believers are blind because of an accident, while others lost their eyesight to spiritual disease and sickness. Vision is precious. It should be protected at all costs. We need to guard our hearts "*lest there be in any of you an evil heart of unbelief, in departing from the living God. But exhort one another daily, while it is called Today; lest any of you be hardened through the deceitfulness of sin.*[21] Unbelief, departure from God, and being beguiled by the deceitfulness of sin will induce blindness every time.

If we are not seeing what others are seeing in the kingdom of God, we need to mimic the action of blind Bartimaeus and cry, "*Lord, that I might receive my sight.*"[22] If we don't get our spiritual eyes healed, we will be disqualified from the priesthood—not as a penalty, but as a perception of an inability to serve God to the people.

A Lame Person Is Disqualified From Serving As A Priest

The second physical blemish that disqualified a candidate was lameness. This does not refer to a limp, but to a total inability to walk. In biblical times, lameness was an incapacitating affliction. They lacked wheelchairs or prosthetic devices to give mobility to the disabled person. The lame were totally dependant upon friends and relatives to carry them from place to place.

Of what value would a priest be if he lacked mobility? It would take at least two other priests to carry him, and that would not be labor efficient.

I have met pastors who were spiritually lame. They could not seem to walk in the things of God. They were totally dependent upon their "intercessory prayer group" to get them into the things of God. They got their sermon material from them and leaned on them for spiritual guidance in the day-to-day activities of the church. They had to be carried in every spiritual realm. They may have been good leaders, fine organizers, and even good speakers, but they were lame and always ended up where their "friends" took them. Such pastors were not followers of God, but were followers of God's people. Who was actually the leader?

If the priest cannot walk the walk, how can he or she lead others into it? He may sit on the sidelines in his wheelchair while barking orders at the exhausted workers, but he is not going before his followers as a true shepherd should. He cannot say, "Follow me as I follow Christ." Jesus said of the true spiritual shepherd, "*when he putteth forth his own sheep, he goeth before them, and the sheep follow him: for they know his voice.*"[23]

The Bible tells followers, "*Remember your leaders, who spoke the word of God to you. Consider the outcome of their way of life and imitate their faith.*"[24] Can a person who is unable to walk the Christian walk ask others to follow him and to imitate his faith? Unfortunately, it happens. Perhaps the group should call themselves the immobilized church of the lame. Their slogan could be, "We specialize in Christian wheelchair cases."

Whatever the cause of lameness, the condition can be cured. Jesus healed many lame persons during His time on earth. The prophet Isaiah, foreseeing the day of Christ's visitation, wrote: "*Then will the lame leap like a deer, and the mute tongue shout for joy. Water will gush forth in the wilderness and streams in the desert.*"[25]

Lameness—an inability to walk—will disqualify us from priestly ministry, but Jesus is the healer of lameness. We can bring it to Him and by faith, walk out as the man at the pool of Bethesda did. We can "*take up thy bed, and walk*" [26] back into the ways of God—meeting needs in the lives of others rather than depending on others to meet the need in our life.

A Person Who Has A Spiritually Flat Nose Is Disqualified From Serving As a Priest.

Whether this refers to the nose or the ability of the nose to discern odors is debatable. Translators take different views. Both concepts hold great spiritual lessons for believer priests.

Consider first the nose that cannot detect odors. God used a special fragrance in the holy oil that anointed the priest and the instruments of worship. He also had a special compounded fragrance in the incense that was burned on the altar in the Holy Place. God specifically prohibited any Israelite from compounding either of these fragrances for personal use under the penalty of death.

Who but a priest would be able to tell if an Israelite had violated this rule? When the worshiper came to offer his sacrifice, the priest took a sniff of his garments. If they smelled like the garments of the priest, the petitioner was interrogated. If, indeed, he had compounded a counterfeit of God's fragrance, he was to be taken out and stoned. You see, that fragrance on the clothing indicated that the person had been in the Holy Place around the incense of God. God didn't want persons pretending they had been there when they had not.

The spiritual implication is quite clear. The book of Revelation declares that the smoke on the Altar of Incense is "*the prayers of the saints*." [27] Few things are more detestable to God than to have persons pretend or declare that they have been in prayer when they haven't been close to the Golden Altar. A believer priest with a flat nose, one that cannot smell, would never know that the worshiper was faking it.

The believer priest without the ability to smell would not realize when something was "fishy." He would not discern the work of demons, and would likely not even know the difference between fleshly and spiritual responses. Too many leaders take what they see as real without ever discerning with their spiritual noses that the whole thing stinks of flesh.

An unsmelling nose also affects the ability to taste. How could a priest with a flat nose "*taste and see that the LORD is good*"?

His ability to appreicate the things of God would be extremely limited. If he cannot sense them, he could never make them real to others.

Furthermore, if he could not taste, how could he know the offerings brought were properly prepared?

Some other translators feel that the Hebrew construction in this verse is concerned with disfiguration—that is the way the New International Version of the Bible translates this verse. The New King James Bible uses the expression "*marred face*."

Since the priest was constantly a representation of God, those who had disfigured faces tended to give a distorted image of God, so they were barred from service. What image of God do we project? Do others, from looking at us, see God as harsh, greedy, lustful, selfish, or even unsmiling? Where we have not become like Jesus, followers tend to see Jesus to be like us. That is sufficient grounds for disqualification from priesthood. Just as Jesus came as a representative of God, so He wants us to represent Him. When we consistently display in our face something that is never on the face of Jesus, we become poor representatives of Christ.

A Person Who Had Anything Superfluous Was Disqualified From Serving As A Priest

This eighteenth verse of Leviticus 21 adds the additional blemish of "*anything that is superfluous.*" The NIV uses the word "*deformed*," while the NKJV says "*a man who has any limb too long*." The implication seems to be that the priest should not have anything about his body that drew attention to himself. God, not the priest, was to be the center of attraction.

Sometimes in the religious arena we see such a display of flesh that God isn't even in the picture. All projections seem to be, "Look at me." It is often difficult to see beyond the costumes, the style of presentation, and the ego-centeredness of one who claims to be "ministering." The words they use may speak of Jesus, but the flesh they display grabs our attention and holds it.

We believer priests need to learn that we represent another; not ourselves. We are giving the message of another; not our own message. We are servants; not the one being served. It is not important that we be seen, but it is important that Jesus be seen and heard through us.

Too much flesh. Disqualified! How memory serves to remind us of many who came on the scene like a shooting star, but faded from sight almost as rapidly as they appeared. The ministers who remain visible are more like the moon that consistently reflects the beauty and glory of the sun.

The great apostle Paul wrote: "*But God forbid that I should glory, save in the cross of our Lord Jesus Christ, by whom the world is crucified unto me, and I unto the world.*"[29] Isn't it likely that when we glory in anything other than the finished work of Christ in our lives that we are growing a leg or arm too long? If so, we may find ourselves disqualified from serving as believer priests. We are not what we are or where we are by any works of our righteousness. We are positioned by divine grace, and that should be both our projection and our boasting. No one should look at us as an abnormality. What we have become in Jesus they, too, can become. We are but normal everyday persons to whom Christ has been revealed.

A Person With A Disabled Foot Is Disqualified From Serving As A Priest

The fifth physical defect that God mentions is "*a man that is brokenfooted.*" This lameness is not a birth defect. The foot was once normal, but it got broken. It is an injury that did not heal properly. How many would-be priests have been injured in their walk with God? Something crushed their foot. Sometimes it was people they tried to help. Other times it was the result of stumbling over something they should have stepped over. Other times it was the result of deliberately stepping from the path of righteousness to the path of sin as Adam did.

The issue is not so much that the priest broke his foot. That happens to many who dare to walk—especially to those who dare to walk the unfamiliar pathway. The problem is that steps were not taken to cause this wound to heal properly. Maybe they refused to acknowledge the break and continued to walk on, ignoring the pain. Christian leaders are notorious for pretending that there is nothing wrong with them. They ignore warning signs in their marriages, hide their heads in the sand when their children get out of order, and refuse to listen to the cry of their bodies to slow down and catch their breath. The foot will probably heal eventually, but it will leave them permanently disabled.

Some Christians who break a foot refuse to turn to another for healing help. They feel ashamed of the break, or feel so self-sufficient they don't want another to know about their disabling wound. They don't even want another to pray for them. It may leave them with a disabled walk into eternity.

Still other wounded priests harbor unforgiveness toward the person who broke their foot. This causes the break to fester and prevent the bones from knitting properly.

We may be willing to put up with a priest who has a defect in his walk, but God isn't. He is willing and able to heal that break, but if the priest is unwilling to be healed, he is disqualified from further service.

A Brokenhanded Person Is Disqualified From Serving As A Priest

The situation here is similar to the brokenfooted person. It is not a birth defect; it is a wound that did not heal properly. Whereas the broken foot prevented the priest from standing in the presence and service of God, the person with a broken hand is greatly limited in his or her service for God.

The priesthood in the time of Moses was very service intensive. The priests actually acted as the butchers for all of Israel, for all animals were to be slain before the Lord. There was an awful lot of slaying, skinning, flaying, and sprinkling of blood. A priest with a broken hand would be too handicapped to perform his duties.

How can we as believer priests reach out to help others if our hand is broken or disabled from a previous break? We would be hard-pressed to present a wave offering before the Lord or to lift the meal offering unto God.

Wouldn't a brokenhanded priest have difficulty offering incense unto God? God's provision was that every time a priest went into the Holy Place, for any reason whatsoever, he was to take a handful of incense and sprinkle it on the coals that were smoldering on the Golden Altar. This produced a cloud of fragrant smoke that filled both the Holy Place and the Holy of Holies. It was praise in its highest form. How very little incense a broken hand can hold. It is likely that the brokenhanded person will be a very limited praiser, and perhaps will be a **worse** giver, for he can hold nothing in his hand.

When Jesus was here, He healed the man with a withered hand. He would still like to do that. He wants His priests to have hands as whole and helpful as His. If we won't bring those broken hands to Him, we may find ourselves disqualified from priestly service.

A Person Who Has A Spiritual Crookback Is Disqualified From Serving As A Priest

The seventh disqualifying defect is called "*crookback*" in the King James Bible, but other translations use the word "*hunchback.*" This is probably more descriptive of the true condition. It is a person who can't stand straight. They are consistently stooped over. Their eyes are perpetually toward the ground. They lack the upward look.

Not only are they seen as an oddity or abnormality, their walk is distorted and they have great difficulty bearing burdens.

We must remember that one of the special tasks for the Old Testament priests in the days of Moses was to transport the tabernacle from camp site to camp site. Most of this was carried on the backs of the priests.

This was decidedly true of the Ark of the Covenant. God provided that this piece that represented the living presence of the Lord be carried by slipping poles through loops and the chosen priests lifting it to their shoulders and walking it from place to place. David learned the hard way that God would accept no shortcut, no matter how ornate the cart may be.

God desires a priesthood that can carry the presence of the Lord on their shoulders. If we cannot stand upright, we cannot take our place in line with other believer priests to carry the ark of God's presence into the midst of God's people.

We also do well to remember the admonition of the Bible: "*Bear ye one another's burdens, and so fulfil the law of Christ.*"[30] While the ultimate burden bearer is the Lord Jesus Christ, we believer priests often need to help others who are crushed under the weight of the sin or personal problems to give their burdens to Jesus. All burdens seem lighter when two or more persons are bearing them. The person with a deformed back is automatically disqualified from this service, for it is impossible for him to be a burden bearer.

The Person Who Is A Spiritual Dwarf Is Also Disqualified From Serving As A Priest

This person had a natural birth, but did not grow up to full stature. Something stunted his or her growth. Sometimes it is disease and other times it is a genetic distortion. Often the mind and organs of the body mature correctly, but the body remains child-sized.

I have been around a few dwarfs and have found them to be very pleasant people. One I knew in particular was a very dedicated Christian and was very proficient in computers. However, all furniture was too large for him. He couldn't reach light switches and the wash basins were hopelessly out of his reach. He was forever having to cope just to live a natural life.

There are Christian believers much like this. They have never matured to the full stature of Christ. They are intellectually normal, but nothing else is. Everything remains out of reach to them. They struggle just to function in the adult Christian world.

Peter urges the believers, "*But grow in grace, and in the knowledge of our Lord and Saviour Jesus Christ. To him be glory both now and for ever. Amen.*" [31] The Christian life is a progressive development. No one is born again in full maturity. This same writer said, "*As newborn babes, desire the sincere milk of the word, that ye may grow thereby.*" [32] Is it possible that bypassing the milk of the Word stunts the growth of some believers? Instead of desiring the milk of the Word, some have despised it. They wanted meat before they had the maturity to digest it. Paul wrote:

> *And **he gave** some, apostles; and some, prophets; and some, evangelists; and some, pastors and teachers; **For the perfecting of the saints,** for the work of the ministry, for the edifying of the body of Christ: **Till we all come** in the unity of the faith, and of the knowledge of the Son of God, **unto a perfect man, unto the measure of the stature of the fulness of Christ: That we henceforth be no more children,** tossed to and fro, and carried about with every wind of doctrine, by the sleight of men, and cunning craftiness, whereby they lie in wait to deceive; But speaking the truth in love**, may grow up into him in all things,** which is the head, even Christ.*" [3]

God has given the milk of His word and gifted ministers to bring us to the full stature of Christ. Rejection of these ministries may well leave us in a child's body with an adult's mind, but this will disqualify us for ministering as a believer priest. We will become one who needs to receive ministry, not one who can give ministry. If consecrated to the priesthood, we will give a very distorted picture of Jesus. People will only see a baby Jesus in a dwarf-sized believer priest.

A Person Who Has A Spiritual Eye Defect Is Disqualified From Serving As A Priest

This person is not blind. He merely has distorted vision. Perhaps he is nearsighted or lacks side vision. Maybe things are a blur in his vision or he may be color blind. Whatever the cause, he has visual defects that disqualify him from ministry.

How often our spiritual eyes have defects. We may not be able to see in the distance or perhaps we overlook things close at hand. It may be that our focus is faulty or that most things are blurred to us. We are both useless and dangerous in God's service if we cannot see with clear vision.

When Jesus visited Bethsaida, they brought a blind man to him who pleaded that he might receive his sight. Jesus led him out of town, spat in his eyes, put His hands on him and asked him if he could now see. "*And he looked up, and said, I see men as trees, walking. After that he put his hands again upon his eyes, and made him look up: and he was restored, and saw every man clearly.*" [34]

Seeing men as trees was a tremendous improvement over being blind, but it was very defective vision. Jesus wouldn't settle for that and gave the man a second touch.

Many candidates for the believer priest ministry need this second touch. They have a distorted image of God, a warped image of life, a prejudiced image of others, and a grandiose image of themselves. They see only trees and they try to interpret them by what they think they should see. They are dangerous as leaders, deceitful as teachers, and destructive as judges. God says: "Disqualified."

A Person With Spiritual Scurvy Is Disqualified From Serving As A Priest

The King James Version of the Bible calls this defect "*scurvy.*" The Living Bible calls it "*pimples.*" The New King James Bible translates it as "*eczema,*" while the Modern Language Bible calls it "*itch or skin trouble.*" The New International Version of the Bible combines "*scurvy and scabbed*" and calls it "*festering or running sores.*"

At the time the King James Version of the Bible was translated, the word *scurvy* denoted all of the above. It was the great scourge of the sailing vessels, and was very common among sailors. It was a skin disorder that resulted from a lack of vitamin

C. The long voyages in that day required great stores of dried beef, beans, and rice. Fresh vegetables and fruit wouldn't store long enough. After a while, the human system called for the vitamins and minerals these fresh vegetables could have provided.

When I was a boy, I had what the doctors called eczema. Both my legs were filled with open running sores. I wore long stockings in those days, and I remember having to soak my legs in water to get the stockings off, for the sores had run through the stockings—forming scabs outside them. It was a lengthy painful process to get my stockings off, and it left me with running sores on my legs. The only cure the doctors in that town could offer was an ointment or salve we rubbed into the wound. Unfortunately, it did little good. Now medical science knows the problem was in my diet. I had the equivalent of the sailor's scurvy. A good daily dose of vitamins, especially vitamin C, and minerals would have cured my problem.

How many would-be priests in our day have open sores—spiritual eczema as a result of improper spiritual diet. They feed on television, magazines, the Internet, and sports, but they do not regularly feed on God's Word. It produces a deficiency that causes running sores in their skin.

Jesus said, "*Whoever eats my flesh and drinks my blood has eternal life, and I will raise him up at the last day. For my flesh is real food and my blood is real drink. Whoever eats my flesh and drinks my blood remains in me, and I in him. Just as the living Father sent me and I live because of the Father, so the one who feeds on me will live because of me.*" [35]

A Person Who Is A Eunuch Is Disqualified From Serving As A Priest

The King James Version says a man who has "*broken stones*" is prohibited from serving as a priest. The New International Version says "*damaged testicles*," but the New King James Version says "*who is a eunuch.*" The obvious meaning of the Hebrew word is that any man who cannot reproduce himself through childbirth cannot be a priest unto God.

Whatever else this may mean, it does suggest that being in the priesthood was not to be a substitute for God's purpose of creation: "*So God created man in his own image, in the image of God he created him; male and female he created them. God blessed them and said to them, 'Be fruitful and increase in number; fill the earth and subdue it.'* "[36] Reproduction was God's first commandment to Adam and He has not withdrawn it yet.

The raising of children is part of the process of attaining maturity. I told each of my daughters at their wedding that I believed I had learned more from them than they had learned from me. They forced me into manhood. God wants His priests to be fully matured in life so they can help those who are just coming into maturity.

The spiritual lesson in this prohibition is simply that God wants each of us to bring forth a replacement. If we cannot reproduce ourselves in our ministry, there will be no one to take our place when we are moved off the scene.

Across America today there are large, nearly empty auditoriums built to accommodate outstanding ministries in days gone by. Although these individuals drew large crowds, they did not reproduce themselves. They did not train a replacement. When they retired or died, the ministry ceased. Effectively, they functioned as eunuchs.

God wants priests who will bring up "sons" after them. Men and women who will reproduce themselves in the ministry so that the work of the Lord will continue beyond our personal contribution.

Does all this sound strange and legalistic? Of course. It even seems that God was nitpicking, but He wasn't. God wants His believer priests to be complete, whole, unblemished persons. Please note that these defects did not affect their birthright—they continued to be provided for as priests—but they nullified their service to God and the people.

We may well join Paul in crying "*Who is sufficient for these things?*" [37] The answer lies outside us. Paul lovingly wrote the Christians in Thessalonica, "*May God himself, the God of peace, sanctify you through and through. May your whole spirit, soul and body be kept blameless at the coming of our Lord Jesus Christ. The one who calls you is faithful and he will do it.*"[38] God called us in our imperfections, but He makes His perfection available to us. Any defect is removable, for He is the great physician. "*He will do it.*" Hallelujah!

Paul told his spiritual son, Timothy, "*All scripture is given by inspiration of God, and is profitable for doctrine, for reproof, for correction, for instruction in righteousness: That the man of God may be perfect, thoroughly furnished unto all good works.*" [39] This is the means God uses to rid us of these limiting defects—His Word. We should read, ingest, cherish, study, and declare that Word at every opportunity, for being a believer priest has so many wonderful benefits we dare not allow a spiritual blemish to disqualify us.

Chapter 9 Endnotes

1. See 1 Peter 1:17
2. Revelation 5:10
3. Revelation 12:10
4. See Zechariah 3:1-5
5. See John 8:44
6. Numbers 16
7. Romans 8:31
8. 1 Peter 2:9
9. Matthew 22:14
10. Leviticus 21:17
11. Leviticus 21:18-23 (parenthetical numbers added)
12. 1 Corinthians 10:11, *NIV*
13. 2 Peter 1:5-9
14. Matthew 15:14
15. Proverbs 20:12
16. See 2 Corinthians 4:4

17. John 3:3, *NIV*
18. 2 Corinthians 4:4
19. 1 John 1:3
20. Matthew 13:14-16
21. Hebrews 3:12-13
22. Mark 10:51
23. John 10:4
24. Hebrews 13:7, *NIV*
25. Isaiah 35:6, *NIV*
26. John 5:11
27. See Revelation 8:3-4
28. Psalm 34:8
29. Galatians 6:14
30. Galatians 6:2
31. 2 Peter 3:18
32. 1 Peter 2:2
33. Ephesians 4:11-15, emphasis added
34. Mark 8:24-25
35. John 6:54-57, *NIV*
36. Genesis 1:27-28, *NIV*
37. 2 Corinthians 2:16
38. 1 Thessalonians 5:23-24, *NIV*
39. 2 Timothy 3:16-17

10
The Entitlement of the Priesthood
The Believer Priest's Privilege

It is sad to realize, as we just saw in the previous chapter, that believer priests can be born to the office, trained for the service, and still be disqualified because of character defects. These men were not removed from the priesthood, they simply were not allowed to serve. They were taken care of for the rest of their lives and they ate the priestly food, but they had no ministry.

What is even worse is to see accepted priests disqualified from further service unto God because they prostituted their priestly ministry. Ezekiel 44 paints a gloomy picture of priests who choose to serve people the way they wanted to be served instead of following God's pattern. They joined the people in idolatry and performed divine rituals to pagan Gods. Their motivation for this is not stated in the Bible, but it is probably the same motivation that causes modern priests to accommodate the way their parishioners want to worship (and whom they desire to worship)—the three "P's": the paycheck, the parsonage, and the pension.

God said, *"The Levites that are gone away far from me, when Israel went astray, which went astray away from me after their idols; they shall even bear their iniquity. Yet they shall be ministers in my sanctuary, having charge at the gates of the house, and ministering to the house: they shall slay the burnt offering and the sacrifice for the people, and they shall stand before them to minister unto them."*[1]

Their choice became their punishment. They had chosen to minister to the people the way they wanted to be ministered to, so God restricted their ministry to *"they shall stand before them to minister unto them."* There was a prohibition that accompanied this punishment. God said, *"And they shall not come near unto me, to do the office of a priest unto me, nor to come near to any of my holy things, in the most holy place: but the shall bear their shame, and their abominations which they have committed."*[2]

How tragic to be chosen, called, and qualified to minister unto God and end up restricted to ministering to the whims of a fickle group of religious people who do not want to serve God.

In contrast to these Levite priests, we read: *"But the priests the Levites, the sons of Zadok, that kept the charge of my sanctuary when the children of Israel went astray from me, they shall come near to me to minister unto me, and they shall stand before me to offer unto me the fat and the blood, saith the Lord GOD: They shall enter into my sanctuary, and they shall come near to my table, to minister unto me, and they shall keep my charge."*[3] What a glorious contrast! The faithful priests were promoted to ministry unto the Lord. They stood before Him, feasted with Him, and ministered worship and praise unto the Lord.

It is this level of ministry we have in mind when we speak of believer priests. God offers special entitlements to those priests who stay with the Word and maintain a pure ministry through the years.

The Priesthood Is Chosen by God

Remembering that Paul told us, *"All these things happened to them as examples-as object lessons to us . . . they were written down so that we could read about them and learn from them in these last days as the world nears its end,"* [4]we dare to look at the priesthood as God established it through Moses in the wilderness. This is the divine pattern and it has spiritual implications for New Testament believers. It is the way God wanted His priesthood to be and God has *"an unchangeable priesthood"*[5] in Christ Jesus. Isn't it likely that He wants an unchangeable priesthood in His Church on earth?

The solemnity with which God placed the original priesthood into office made it obvious to all Israel that the priesthood was a calling of God, not a choosing of men. It was a consecration far more than a profession. It was entered by birth, not by education—the education came later.

Believer priests are chosen by God. Jesus told His disciples who were undergoing training to be priests unto God, "You *did not choose me, but I chose you and appointed you to go and bear fruit—fruit that will last."*[6] The same is true of us. The Lord chose us. We testify to having chosen Jesus, but actually we merely chose to accept His choice. We were lost and He found us. We were bound by sin and He loosed us. We were carnal self-centered individuals and He has made us spiritual beings who are Christ-centered. We were penitent sinners and He chose to make us a royal priesthood. Our priesthood is one hundred percent dependent upon His choices, but, thank God, He did choose us. Hallelujah!

God chose us to be different. Paul encouraged the church at Corinth to remember that they were not normal people because of the work of Christ in their lives. Paul urged them that they not walk as "normal" people. Whatever "normal" is may be all right for the world, but believer priests are abnormal. We march to a different drum beat—one that we hear in our spirit. This does not serve notice on the world that we want nothing to do with commerce and trade. That's foolish. We're in the world, but we're not of it. We have learned by the grace of God how to maintain a meter; a beat that the world does not hear. We have an understanding that character in life is important, and that we are responsible for attitude and character as we live as believer priests in the grace of God.

There are, obviously, some inherent restrictions that go along with being a believer priest. The priest is called to a different life style, for ministry unto the Lord requires a life of separation unto the Lord. Some persons feel that the exclusions imposed on a believer priest are overly severe, but they have failed to see the amazing entitlements made available to the priest who will separate himself or herself to ministering unto the Lord. What we receive is so much greater than what we relinquish.

There are glorious privileges available to the one who will serve God acceptably. I remember when I was a boy that so many of the guest ministers who stood in my father's pulpit emphasized what they had "given up" to serve the Lord. It formed a very negative impression about being a minister. The Christians of that day picked up this projected message and their testimonies often dwelt on what they had sacrificed to be a Christian. It often sounded like the price for being a servant of God was exceedingly high. The truth is, we don't even pay the sales tax on the product. God always gives more abundantly than He takes from us.

I don't want to minimize the fact that the Cross exerts a price, but compared to what Christ sacrificed for us, what can we actually give up for His sake that can even enter a comparison equation? Is it possible that David was briefly dwelling on the cost of being a believer priest when he commanded his soul to remember the benefits he had received from serving God? He wrote: *"Bless the LORD, 0 my soul: and all that is within me, bless his holy name. Bless the LORD, 0 my soul,* ***and forget not all his benefits."***[7]

There is no endeavor in life that does not call for some sacrifice. Look at our athletes giving so many hours a day to training. They don't have enough time left to live a "normal life," but for them the benefits outweigh the sacrifices. Paul reminds us, "No *one serving as a soldier gets involved in civilian affairs—he wants to please his commanding officer.*" [8]Most professions force restrictions on the participants, but the rewards far exceed the restrictions.

It is similar for believer priests, but there are multiple rewards for every encumbrance. God is the perfect Father. He doesn't snatch playthings from us. He offers us something far better. As we reach out to claim it, we gladly cast aside the lesser thing.

Peter understood that God's priests are distinctly different in life. He wrote: *"But you are not like that, for* ***you have been chosen by God himself****—you are priests of the King, you are holy and pure,* ***you are God's very own****—all this so that you may show to others how God called you out of the darkness into his wonderful light."*[9] Peter assures us that we have been **chosen** by God, **changed** by God, made **children** of God, and **commissioned** by God, and these are but beginning entitlements to priesthood.

The Priesthood Entitles Us to Separation Unto God

Deep in the spirit of men and women, both regenerated and unregenerated persons, is a deep craving for nearness to God. It is as inborn as a hunger for food or a craving for sexual fulfillment. God made us to need Him, and God has never created a need without also creating a fulfillment for that need. To satisfy our craving for Him, God has made Himself fully available to us. All may enjoy a measure of the presence of God, for part of our salvation is the indwelling of the Holy Spirit.

Believer priests have a special separation unto God, for God calls them to Himself much as He separated the Levites from the encampment in the wilderness and had them pitch their tents around the tabernacle. This, obviously, made them more accessible to the work of the tabernacle, but it also separated them from the day-to-day activities of the children of Israel.

Blessed is the Christian servant who recognizes the privilege of being separated to divine service. This is especially true of the full-time servant of God and the Church. He or she is not involved in the hurry-scurry of the commercial world. God has provided support for their ministry, and they can give themselves to study, prayer, ministry, and enjoying the presence of God. This is a bonus from the hand of God that should not be abused. God did not encamp the Levites around the tabernacle to be inactive and lazy. They had much work to do, but their work was in the service of the Lord. When they had fulfilled their daily term of activity, they could enjoy being near the presence of God.

Even believer priests who support themselves and still minister unto God have the entitlement to separation unto God. When Jesus prayed to the Father about His disciples (the early believer priests), He said, *"They are not of the world, even as I am not of the world."*[10] We are in the world system, but we are not a part of it. We function as ambassadors of Christ in this world, but we are not a part of the world. We are miniature representatives of the heavenly country where we have our citizenship. Our homes are embassies of heaven. We have immunity conferred on us by right of being representatives of the heavenly realm. We are separated unto God even while being involved with business in the world.

This separation was mandatory for the Old Testament priests. Even the Aaronic priests were encamped abound the tabernacle; completely separated unto God. Unfortunately, many believer priests of the New Testament era seem to feel that this extreme separation is optional. Perhaps they have overlooked the declared imperative: *"Therefore come out from them and be separate, says the Lord. Touch no unclean thing, and I will receive you. I will be a Father to you, and you will be my sons and daughters, says the Lord Almighty."*[11] This is a call from the Spirit of God. It is not an option; it is an obligation. If we would serve as priests, we must be separated unto God.

In light of this, Paul, the channel through whom the Holy Spirit was writing, adds, *"Since we have these promises, dear friends, let us purify ourselves from everything that contaminates body and spirit, perfecting holiness out of reverence for God."*[12]

This call to separation is such a privilege and offers such benefits to the believer priest that it is little wonder our mortal enemy tries to make this separation seem like a negative. Satan would like us to believe that we are missing out on real life, when in fact, we have been invited to participate in the life of Christ-eternal life-that offers hope, joy, relationship with God, and a glorious fellowship with fellow believer priests. We are invited to trade shadows for substance, pretense for reality, and the workings of death for the workings of life. How could this possibly be viewed as a negative?

Perhaps we believer priests need to look beyond the call to separate from and grasp the reality that our entitlement is separation unto. Separation unto God! Separated unto hearing God speak as we read His Word. Separated unto communication with God through prayer. Separated to working together with the Lord. What a holy calling! What a privilege! What an entitlement!

Throughout the Bible, the men and women God used were first separated unto God. It is obvious in the priesthood, but it was just as evident in the initial kingly offices. David was especially sought out and separated to divine service. David was a specialist in tending sheep, but God chose him to become a shepherd of Israel. To do so, David had to leave his father's sheep and undergo training to fulfill God's higher calling.

The prophets of the Old Testament were persons called to a separated life. At times, that separation marked them as odd individuals. Often their lifestyles were so different that just looking at them made it evident that they were prophets. Much as is said of Enoch, they *"walked with God."*[13] In times of apostasy when few persons had a relationship with God, these individuals walked in their separation and fellowshiped with the voice of God. They were living representatives of God to their generations.

We are living in another age of apostasy. In spite of our reputation, it takes a stretch of the imagination to call America a Christian nation any more. God is calling individuals to walk out of the American culture into the culture of Christ and be faithful witnesses to the reality of God, salvation, and heaven. This is far more than a mental decision; it is a lifestyle. God wants American believer priests, who have accepted the call to separation unto God, who can be *"witnesses unto me."*[14]

The Priesthood Entitles Us to Relationship With God

It is possible to be set aside for a person and still have no personal relationship with him or her. The secret service agents who guard our president may be near him, but they have no true personal relationship with him. That is not a perk of their job.

It seems that too many Christians who accept the entitlement of being close to the Lord fail to accept the perk of having a relationship with Him. We have not been invited into His household as servants. We are family. We have been urged to leave our tents in the general encampment and pitch it on the Father's property.

Israel saw the entire area of the tabernacle as sacred territory. They visualized it as the place where God dwelt. Only the High Priest could enter the Holy of Holies where God's presence was actualized between the faces of the Cherubim on the Mercy Seat. The High Priest could come there only on the day of atonement. Even being allowed to come into the Holy Place to burn the incense was seen as having very intimate fellowship with God. This was the entitlement of the Aaronic priests. The Levitical priests were restricted to the Outer Court of the tabernacle, but that was a great deal closer to God than the members of Israel ever dared to approach God.

We are familiar with the expression, "Rank has its privileges." This is as true in the kingdom of God as in military service. Those who have responded to God's call to encamp around His tabernacle have privileges unavailable to those who prefer to remain in the outer camp. We who have encamped close to the Lord have an intimate relationship with God made available to us.

The Song of Solomon illustrates this. There were many

"virgins" who loved the king, but it was the Shulamite maiden who cried, *"Draw me . . . the king hath brought me into his chambers."*[15] She was willing to forsake her own vineyard to pursue this king, and the consistent cry of her heart was *"Draw me."* It was she, not the others, who ended up married to the king.

We dare not allow ourselves to be satisfied with pitching our tents outside the linen walls of the tabernacle. We have been invited to come closer. We're slated for an intimate relationship with the Lord. He wants more than our service, He wants our love. He has provided an entrance from our tents to His. We are admonished, *"Let us then approach the throne of grace with confidence, so that we may receive mercy and find grace to help us in our time of need."*[16] Our confidence is not in ourselves, but in His invitation-His provision. If He says to come in, we have the right to do so.

When I was a pastor, members of my church usually needed an appointment to see me and had to come through my secretary to enter my office. My daughters, however, were free to come in at any time with little more than a polite knock on the door as they turned the doorknob. What was the difference? Relationship and provision. I was pastor to several hundred persons, but I was father to only three girls. Those girls had a relationship with me that no member of my congregation would ever know, and out of that relationship came special privileges.

We are far more than members of God's great congregation of believers. We are sons and daughters of God. John informs us, *"Beloved, now are we the sons of God, and it doth not yet appear what we shall be: but we know that, when he shall appear, we shall be like him; for we shall see him as he is."*[17] We are sons that serve as part of a family priesthood. We minister unto Him, but we also have an intimate relationship with Him.

God refers to the priests as *"My priests,"*[18] and the New Testament says, *"You are God's very own."*[19] This establishes once and for all our right to a relationship with God. It is by His action, not ours. It was His choice, not ours. We don't create the relationship, we respond to or reject it.

The Priesthood Entitles Us to Fellowship With God

On the surface, having relationship with God would seem to be synonymous to enjoying fellowship with Him, but even life teaches us that this is not necessarily so. Many children, though rightly related to their fathers, live their entire lives at home without enjoying fellowship with their dads. They share the same house, the same name, the same provisions, but there was a consistent distance between father and the children, A family survey recently revealed that the average businessman spends less than ten minutes a day with his children. We could hardly call that fellowship.

Isn't it obvious that many believer priests spend less than ten minutes daily with their Heavenly Father? Much of those ten minutes are cold and formal business minutes.

We do well to remember that God's desire in creating Adam and Eve was for personal fellowship with them. The three of them walked in the cool of the evening in sweet communion, until sin separated them. As we saw in chapter one, God instituted the sacrificial system to restore a small portion of this fellowship between Himself and His special creatures. When He instituted the priestly system, He chose the priests as representatives of the people. In fellowshiping with the priests, God was, by identification, fellowshiping with His people.

Oh, how God longs for priests who will talk to Him. Through the prophet Jeremiah, God pleads, *"Call to me and I will answer you and tell you great and unsearchable things you do not know."*[20] He wants men and women whose minds are open to hear the voice of God; persons to whom heavenly values exceed earthly values, and who understand spiritual things. Believer priests do not need to talk God into having fellowship with them. God is far more anxious for this intimate fellowship than the priests are.

Paul not only enjoyed this fellowship with God, but projected the availability of that fellowship to all of us. He wrote: "God, *who has called you into fellowship with his Son Jesus Christ our Lord, is faithful."*[21] Believer priests are not only called to fellowship one another, they are invited to fellowship with God's Son, Jesus Christ. Does this seem awesome? It is, but it is actual. God bids us to enjoy times of friendship with Jesus.

These times of fellowship are made available to us through faith in God's offer, not through works of our righteousness. No one deserves this level of fellowship, but all believer priests can enjoy it. James says of Abraham, *"Abraham believed God, and it was imputed unto him for righteousness: and he was called the Friend of God."*[22] Similarly, we can dare to believe God means it when He invites us to share open friendship with His Son. It is one of the entitlements of the priesthood.

The Priesthood Entitles Us to Offer Service Unto God

The Psalmist speaks for all of us when he wrote, *"How can I repay the LORD for all his goodness to me*?"[23] We humans can receive from one another only to a point where our sense of obligation requires us to do in turn, or refuse to allow anything further to be done for us. God who made us knows this well, so He offers His believer priests a chance to give back to Him something that discharges our sense of indebtedness.

It is self-evident that nothing we do can truly repay the Lord for what He has done. What kind of payment can we make for the Cross? We are not trying to pay a debt or get even, we're merely giving something useful to the Lord as an offering of thanks for the great gift of eternal life He has given to us. Three times the Bible urges us, *"Give unto the LORD the glory due unto his name."*[24] This rendering of adoration is special to God and a delight to us.

If we have come this far in presenting the truth that the fundamental ministry of a believer priest is to worship God and help others to worship Him, I have failed to communicate well. Everything we do must flow out of our worship of the Lord. It is always worship first; work second. It is out of our praise to God that we perform our service as believer priests. Nothing, absolutely nothing, dare become a substitute for worship.

This is the greatest entitlement God has granted a believer priest—we have the right and responsibility to initiate worship personally and publicly. We should be prepared to praise the Lord everywhere, in every way, and every moment.

Praise, however, is not the only service the believer priest can offer to God. Remember that the service of the Levitical priesthood was on behalf of the people unto God. All sacrifices had to be offered by the priests. Their duties were laborious and continuous. They had the continual care of the tabernacle. Furthermore, they dismantled and moved it from place to place and reassembled it at the new camp site as God led Israel through the wilderness.

All of this service was liturgical service—ministry done on God's behalf. Depending on the attitude of the priest, it was a duty or a delight, but it was declared to be a ministry unto God.

The Priesthood Entities Us to Serve God to the People

How easy it is to forget that all liturgical service is ultimately unto God. It often seems that we are giving ourselves to people and their problems, but everything we do as believer priests is accepted as ministry unto God. Jesus said: *"Inasmuch as ye have done it unto one of the least of these my brethren, ye have done it unto me."*[25]

In a most wonderful way, we are encouraged to not only serve God, but to actually serve God to the people. The Old Testament priest not only ceremonially lifted the people and their needs to God, he ministered God's grace and forgiveness to the people. He became an intermediary between the people and their God. If that is our example, let's follow it.

Believer priests can become channels that bring the reality and presence of God to others. While we would never usurp Christ's position as the mediator between God and man, for the Bible assures us, *"There is one God, and one mediator between*

God and men, the man Christ Jesus,"[26] still believer priests become the downlink from heaven's provision to man's need.

Serving God is very practical. We help others get into the presence of God. Sometimes we are helping them handle a sin problem, and we bring them to the sacrifice of Jesus at Calvary. Other times we are dealing with defilement of earthly living, and we bring them to the Laver of God's Word.

Sometimes we forget that the priests were the teachers of God's Word to the people. We believer priests are also instructors in righteousness for other believers. In the Ezekiel passage referred to earlier, God put a distinction between the function of the priests who joined the people in idol worship and the sons of Zadok who *"kept the charge of my sanctuary."* God said that after these faithful priest had ministered at His table in His presence, they were to return to the outer court, *"And they shall teach my people the difference between the holy and profane, and cause them to discern between the unclean and the clean."*[27]

Only one who knows God can teach God to another. Only the believer priest who has caught a glimpse of a Holy God can explain to others the difference between the holy and the profane. God's believer priests teach from a position of experience, and that type of teaching has tremendous authority.

Many people do not know how to give God a sacrifice of praise, so we must teach them. They know nothing of worship, so we must lead them in worship. We become a demonstration, for we teach far better from example of life than from expression of words.

Two areas where people often need the teaching help of believer priests are in giving thanks and giving substance. People find it far easier to ask from God than to thank God for what they have received. Human memories seem so very short. Priests should help the petitioner to realize that he or she has no right to request more until he or she has said "thank you" for what has been received. The Old Testament order of approach to God was: *"Enter into his gates with thanksgiving, and into his courts with praise:*

be thankful unto him, and bless his name."[28] Just as it is useless to start talking on the phone until the dialed party answers, so it is useless to petition God until we are in His presence, and the gateway to His presence is thanksgiving and praise. It is an entitlement to priests to teach this to people. What a privilege!

Similarly, believer priests need to help other Christians learn that God wasn't hinting when He said, *"Bring ye all the tithes into the storehouse, that there may be meat in mine house, and prove me now herewith, saith the LORD of hosts, if I will not open you the windows of heaven, and pour you out a blessing, that there shall not be room enough to receive it."*[29] It was a command!

In the Old Testament, it was impossible to worship God without bringing a gift, for the sacrifices were supplied by the people. There was no provision for freeloading. There should be no place for it in the New Testament era, either. God wants us to worship Him with the tithes of our income. This is the barest minimum. Beyond this, He calls for love gifts and offerings. Most new believers don't know this. It is a learned experience, and believer priests are the teachers. It is a ministry to the people on God's behalf. Teaching this is liturgical service in God's sight.

David sang, *"Serve the LORD with gladness: come before his presence with singing."*[30] In ministry, we often come to God with the burdens of people, sin problems that need to be forgiven, and burdens of life that need to be lifted. David suggested that we get those negative needs settled as quickly as possible and come into God's presence with songs of rejoicing. God is a happy God who enjoys happy people. We should put a smile on our faces when we come into God's presence. Let the heart leap with joy and the mouth proclaim the praises of Almighty God. Coming into God's presence is celebration time. We are not petitioning for a loan, we're claiming a promise. Our service is far more festivity than religious activity.

God has promised to meet our needs. Isn't it time we meet needs in God by joyfully fellowshiping with Him? He has heard enough moans and groans to last an eternity. Let's give Him the incense of praise and the delight of joyful songs. This is the highest ministry a priest can offer before God-praise and worship, but it has to come out of fellowship, not ritual.

The Priesthood Entitles Us to Ample Provision

When the Levites were chosen to function with the Aaronic priesthood, God made ample provision to maintain their households. They were to receive the tithes of the people and, in turn, to pay tithe of this to sustain Aaron and his sons. They were not asked to live "by faith."

Some years ago, I was a guest in a home of some saints in Australia who were seeking to believe God for their source of supply while they were helping establish a new church in the city. The youngest son responded to his school teacher's question, "What does faith mean?" by answering, "Faith means doing without." I thought that was famine, not faith.

Fundamentally, God established a cycle where the persons ministered to would support the ones who ministered to them. This is still God's provision for His ministers. Paul wrote: *"Don't you know that those who work in the temple get their food from the temple, and those who serve at the altar share in what is offered on the altar? In the same way, the Lord has commanded that those who preach the gospel should receive their living from the gospel."*[31]

We should remember that it is not holding the office that entitles us to support, but working that office. Paul reminded the Thessalonian Christians, *"For even when we were with you, we gave you this rule: 'If a man will not work, he shall not eat.'"*[32] The Levite priests were hard working men, and believer priests should be faithful laborers for their Master.

With this in mind, may I assure you that God is a good pay master. When we faithfully minister, He faithfully provides all things needful both for ministry and for living.

God's first supply is for everything we need to function as a priest. The Levite priests could not offer sacrifices unless they were brought to them. They had no resources of their own. Neither have we. We believer priests need to realize that we lack spiritual resources from which to minister. We may have brilliant minds and ambitious wills, but the ministry we have been called to is a spiritual ministry that requires the provision of God's Holy Spirit. Fortunately, there is no shortage of God's Spirit. He is available to all believer priests in His person, His power, His gifts, and His fruit. He is equal to any occasion or need. Let Him flow through you in ministry.

God's second supply is for every provision we need to function in life. He may not give us all that we want, or all that we think we need, but He will supply all we really need. That was Paul's affirmation to the believer priests in Phillipi: *"But my God shall supply all your need according to his riches in glory by Christ Jesus."*[33]

When faith rises to embrace this entitlement, the stress and worry about money and possessions that so drives the non-believer drops away. Our minds are freed to meditate on God instead of constantly worrying about making money. Anxiety gives way to assurance. Contentment replaces contention, and we minister in the assurance that the Father has everything that we will need to live victoriously in Christ Jesus and to serve Him as a believer priest.

The Priesthood Is Entitled to a Glorious Inheritance

When the second generation of Hebrews went into the Promised Land and conquered the territory, Joshua divided the land and distributed it by lots to the tribes as their perpetual inheritance. The tribe of Levi was exempted by divine decree. They were given cities in these various areas for their residence, but these were also "cities of refuge" where one, who accidentally slew another, could flee to seek asylum.

Some have wondered why God didn't give massive farms to these faithful ministers of the sanctuary, but God knew they would not have time to tend them. Their service was to be unto the Lord. How much better off the full-time believer priests would be if we would stop trying to build a fortune by dabbling in what has become the inheritance of others, and just give ourselves wholly to the work of the Lord.

If exempting the priestly Levites from receiving an inheritance with the other eleven tribes seems unfair, please remember that God said, *"I am to be the only inheritance the priests have. You are to give them no possession in Israel; I will be their possession."*[34] What a trade off. Israel got land while the priests got God!

Believer priests are offered this same divine inheritance. God offers to be our possession. What glorious protection this gives us. He promises, *"I will be an enemy to your enemies and will oppose those, who oppose you."*[35] Just as I never feared the school bully when I was walking hand in hand with my father, I need not fear anything in the spirit world when God offers to be an enemy to my enemies. This is part of my entitled inheritance.

Having God as our heritage assures us of His constant presence. He told Joshua, *"I will be with you; I will never leave you nor forsake you,"*[36] and the New Testament assures us, *"God has said, 'Never will I leave you; never will I forsake you. 'So we say with confidence, 'The Lord is my helper; I will not be afraid What can man do to me?'"*[37] We don't come into His presence three times a year during the compulsory feasts as the children of Israel did. We have a constant abiding of God in our lives. This is our inheritance as believer priests.

All persons are subject to times of trouble, but the believer priest has as part of his inheritance the promise, "I will *be with him in trouble; I will deliver him, and honour him.*"[38] There are many other *"I will be . . ."* promised in the Word. When we have God as our inheritance, we have all that He is, all that He has, and all that He offers to us. Who could possibly need more than this?

Please remember that if God is our inheritance, we share His home. Jesus promised that He was going to prepare a place for us in heaven. The beautiful New Jerusalem with its streets of gold, gates of pearl, tree of life, and living water will be our place of residence. We will enjoy the glad praises of the angels, and the anthems of great choirs of redeemed persons. We'll experience the absence of sickness, pain, sorrow, death, and defilement. Eternal joy will spring up in our spirits. The holiness of God will permeate the atmosphere of our lives.

In the Father's house, as Jesus called heaven, we'll be reunited with loved ones who went on before us. We'll be able to share experiences with Abraham, Moses, David, Esther, Deborah, and other great men and women of the Bible. We'll live in the realized presence of Jesus forever.

What an inheritance! What a reward for faithful believer priests! Our entitlements are far richer than our imaginations can conceive. Paul said so when he wrote: "No *eye has seen, no ear has heard, no mind has conceived what God has prepared for those who love him—but God has revealed it to us by his Spirit.*"[39] Whatever these things may be, if they are God's, they are ours, for He is our inheritance.

Chapter 10 Endnotes

1. Ezekiel 44:10-11
2. Ezekiel 44:13
3. Ezekiel 44:15-16
4. 1Corinthians 10:11, *TLB*
5. Hebrews 7:24
6. John 15:16, *NIV*
7. Psalm 103:1-2, emphasis added
8. 2 Timothy 2:4, *NIV*

9. 1 Peter 2:9, TLB, emphasis added

10. John 17:14

11. 2 Corinthians 6:17-18, *NIV*

12. 2 Corinthians 7:1

13. Genesis 5:24

14. Acts 2:4

15. Song of Solomon 1:4

16. Hebrews 4:16, *NIV*

17. 1 John 3:2

18. Lamentations 1:19

19. 1 Peter 2:9, *TLB*

20. Jeremiah 33:3, *NIV*

21. 1 Corinthians 1:9, *NIV*

22. James 2:23

23. Psalm 116:12, *NIV*

24. 1 Chronicles 16:29; Psalm 29:2, 96:8

25. Matthew 25:40

26. 1 Timothy 2:5

27. Ezekiel 44:23

28. Psalm 100:4

29. Malachi 3:10

30. Psalm 100:2

31. 1 Corinthians 9:13-14

32. 2 Thessalonians 3:10, *NIV*

33. Philippians 4:19

34. Ezekiel 44:28, *NIV*

35. Exodus 23:22, *NIV*

36. Joshua 1:5

37. Hebrews 13:5-6

38. Psalm 91:15

39. 1 Corinthians 2:9-10